THE MARRI

Pierre-Augustin Caron de Beaumarchais

THE MARRIAGE OF FIGARO

translated and adapted by

Robert Cogo-Fawcett
and
Braham Murray

OBERON BOOKS
LONDON

WWW.OBERONBOOKS.COM

First published in 2003 by Oberon Books Ltd
521 Caledonian Road, London N7 9RH
Tel: +44 (0) 20 7607 3637 / Fax: +44 (0) 20 7607 3629
e-mail: info@oberonbooks.com
www.oberonbooks.com

A catalogue record for this book is available from the British
Library.

PB ISBN: 978-1-84002-377-0

Cover design by Andrzej Klimowski

Visit www.oberonbooks.com to read more about all our books
and to buy them. You will also find features, author interviews and
news of any author events, and you can sign up for e-newsletters
so that you're always first to hear about our new releases.

Characters

COUNT ALMAVIVA
Governor of Andalucia

THE COUNTESS
his wife

FIGARO
his valet

SUZANNA
the Countess' maid and
Figaro's fiancée

MARCELINE
housekeeper

ANTONIO
head gardener, Suzanna's
uncle and Fanchette's father

FANCHETTE
Antonio's daughter

CHERUBINO
page to the Count

BARTHOLO
a doctor from Seville

BAZILE
the Countess' music master

DON GUISMAN
GOSLING
magistrate

UNDERHAND
clerk of the court

An USHER

SUNBURN
a young shepherd

PEDRILLO
the Count's groom

PEASANTS

This adaptation of *The Marriage of Figaro* was first performed on 27 May 2003 at The Royal Exchange Theatre, Manchester, with the following cast:

COUNT, Simon Robson

COUNTESS, Emma Cunningham

FIGARO, Kulvinder Ghir

SUZANNA, Nina Sosanya

MARCELINE, Carol Ann Crawford

ANTONIO, John Cording

FANCHETTE, Lydia Baksh

CHERUBINO, Samuel Barnett

BARTHOLO, Robert Austin

BAZILE, Glyn Pritchard

GOSLING, John Southworth

UNDERHAND, Andrew Grose

USHER, Chris Hannon

SUNBURN, Chris Hannon

PEDRILLO, Andrew Grose

PEASANTS, Glyn Pritchard, John Cording, Lydia Baksh, Andrew Grose, Chris Hannon, Jo Pridding

Director, Helena Kaut-Howson

Designer, Johanna Bryant

Lighting, Vince Herbert

Composer, Richard Blackford

Sound, Steve Brown

Fights, Renny Krupinski

Choreographer, Jack Murhpy

ACT ONE

A semi-furnished bedroom. There is a large canopied armchair in the middle of the room. FIGARO is measuring the floor with a large rule. SUZANNA is looking at herself in a mirror, weighing up her bride's headdress, a small garland of orange flowers.

FIGARO: Nineteen by twenty-six.

SUZANNA: Don't you think it looks better like this, Figaro?

FIGARO: (*Taking her hands.*) I do, my darling! A virgin's crown for my bride to be, on our wedding day!

SUZANNA: What are you measuring, my boy?

FIGARO: I'm trying to see how his Lordship's present will fit. That lovely bed he's giving us.

SUZANNA: You want it in here?

FIGARO: This is where he suggested.

SUZANNA: It won't do!

FIGARO: What do you mean?

SUZANNA: It's not acceptable, that's all.

FIGARO: But why not?

SUZANNA: I don't like it.

FIGARO: What's the matter with it?

SUZANNA: I don't have to tell you everything.

FIGARO: No…but you do seem to have strong opinions on the subject.

SUZANNA: Can't you just trust me?

FIGARO: But it's the most convenient room in the chateau. It's between the two suites. If her Ladyship needs you in the middle of the night, she rings her bell and you're up and into her quarters in two shakes of a lamb's tail. If the Count wants something, he's only to give a tiny tinkle and abracadabra! a hop, skip and a jump and there I am, at his side.

SUZANNA: Oh yes. And first thing in the morning all his Lordship has to do is to give a tiny tinkle, send you on a long errand and abracadabra! a hop, skip and a jump and in two shakes of his lamb's tail he's at my side!

FIGARO: What are you getting at?

SUZANNA: His Lordship is tired of the local beauties so he's coming home, and not to his wife but to your fiancée. That's what this room is all about. I know! His pimp Bazile told me at our last singing lesson.

FIGARO: Bazile! I'll ram his baton up his backside.

SUZANNA: Did you really think that this dowry his Lordship's giving me was a reward for the services you've rendered?

FIGARO: But I've put myself on the line for him.

SUZANNA: Clever men can be very stupid!

FIGARO: I see.

SUZANNA: He wants me on my own for a quarter of an hour.

FIGARO: What for?

SUZANNA: Do you remember the *droit de seigneur*?

FIGARO: The Lord of the Manor's right to bed any bride on their wedding night?

SUZANNA: Precisely.

FIGARO: You don't mean?

SUZANNA: At last!

FIGARO: But he abolished it when he married the Countess.

SUZANNA: He's missing it and he's planning a revival with me.

FIGARO: My head's spinning! (*Rubbing his forehead.*) There must be a way of foiling him, trapping him and fleecing him!

SUZANNA: Cash and conspiracy! You're in your element.

FIGARO: Hang on a minute…

SUZANNA: Are you afraid?

FIGARO: Of course not. I'm thinking! Taking risks is no problem but to escape with a proper reward is the point. If I could…

(*A bell rings off.*)

SUZANNA: That'll be my Lady. She must be awake. I have to be the first to speak to her on my wedding day. She asked me especially.

FIGARO: Any particular reason?

SUZANNA: There's a saying that it brings luck to neglected wives. Goodbye, my little Fi, Fi, Figaro. Don't forget our problem, will you?

FIGARO: What about a kiss to give me courage?

SUZANNA: From my lover? But what would my husband say?

(*FIGARO kisses her.*)

That's enough!

FIGARO: I can't begin to tell you how much I love you.

SUZANNA: (*Smoothing her hair.*) You never stop from morning until night.

FIGARO: (*Secretively.*) And I'll go on until I can prove it to you from night until morning.

The bell rings again.

SUZANNA: (*Fingers on her lips.*) Take your kiss back. There! Now I've got nothing that belongs to you.

FIGARO: (*Running after her.*) But you liked it when I gave it to you.

(*SUZANNA exits.*)

She's a delight! Beautiful, fun, loving – but clever! (*He walks up and down, rubbing his hands.*) So, your Excellency! My dear master! I wondered what you were up to. First you put me in charge of your household. Then you offer to take me with you to England as a courier in your ambassador's retinue. Three promotions: you as the new ambassador; me, the errand boy and Suzie to the ambassador's bed. And while I'm galloping away on my charger with my errands, you're riding my wife! While I'm battling to increase his family's glory he's increasing the size of mine! Well, you've gone too far this time, your Lordship. And as for Bazile! I'll teach him! No, calm down, Figaro! We must keep up a pretence then I'll play off one against the other. Let's see! First of all we'll bring the time of the wedding forward so we can be sure it'll actually take place; next we'll divert Marceline's attention so she'll keep her hands off me; then we'll pocket the dowry and the presents; put his Lordship off the scent; give Bazile a good thrashing and…

(*MARCELINE and BARTHOLO enter.*)

Ah-ha! Here's fat Bartholo. My wedding party wouldn't have been complete without him. Good morning, Doctor. What brings you to the castle? Could it be my impending marriage?

BARTHOLO: (*Disdainfully.*) Certainly not!

FIGARO: Such generosity!

BARTHOLO: Such asinine stupidity!

FIGARO: I suppose it's not surprising given I stopped your marriage to the Countess!

BARTHOLO: Do you have anything else to say?

FIGARO: *Au revoir*, Marceline.

'Out of love and full of hate?'

If you still want to take me to court, may I recommend the doctor.

BARTHOLO: What do you mean?

FIGARO: She'll tell you. (*Exits.*)

BARTHOLO: (*Watching him going.*) He never changes. Arrogant. Insolent.

MARCELINE: (*Turning him round.*) And nor do you. You're the typical doctor. So secretive and self-important the patient can die waiting for a diagnosis. No wonder the Countess eloped with the Count instead of marrying you.

BARTHOLO: As bitter and spiteful as ever, Marceline! Tell me why I'm here? Who requires my presence at the chateau? Has the Count had an accident?

MARCELINE: No doctor.

BARTHOLO: The Countess then? Could the deceitful Rosine be unwell? Heaven be praised!

MARCELINE: She's languishing.

BARTHOLO: From what?

MARCELINE: Neglect. Her husband never comes near her.

BARTHOLO: (*Contentedly.*) I have something to be grateful to him for!

MARCELINE: I don't know what to make of the Count. He's a jealous husband and a lecher at the same time.

BARTHOLO: Lecherous from boredom, jealous from vanity. That's usually the explanation.

MARCELINE: Today for example, he's marrying off Suzanna to his valet Figaro. The union has his blessing.

BARTHOLO: Presumably Suzanna's already had something else from him. Isn't that why there's a wedding?

MARCELINE: Not exactly. But his Excellency wouldn't mind having his own celebration with the bride…

BARTHOLO: I'm sure he could come to an arrangement with Figaro.

MARCELINE: Bazile says not.

BARTHOLO: Is that reptile here too? What a cess pit. What's he up to?

MARCELINE: He's still infatuated with me. It's so boring.

BARTHOLO: I know how you can cure him.

MARCELINE: How?

BARTHOLO: Marry him.

MARCELINE: That's cruel Bartholo when you could have cured me the same way. Well you could, couldn't you? Have you forgotten the fruit of our love? Our long lost Emmanuel. Where is he now? His birth should have meant our marriage.

BARTHOLO: (*Raising his hat.*) Have you brought me all the way from Seville to listen to this twaddle? You're always talking about marriage. If it's so vital to you...

MARCELINE: Alright! We'll drop the subject. But if you won't marry me at least you can listen to my plans for catching somebody else.

BARTHOLO: Which sorry mortal abandoned by God and mankind have you chosen?

MARCELINE: Figaro.

BARTHOLO: That double-crossing thief!

MARCELINE: But he's fun; he's carefree, cheerful, happy-go-lucky. He worries about the future as little as he does about the past; and he's as generous as...

BARTHOLO: ...as a thief.

MARCELINE: as a mogul! He's utterly charming and completely vile. He won't have me.

BARTHOLO: What about Suzanna?

MARCELINE: She's cunning. But she won't get her hands on him. I need your help Doctor. I want to exact the promise he made me.

BARTHOLO: On his wedding day?

MARCELINE: We can stop that nonsense. The most adventurous of our sex has an inner voice which says: if you can, be beautiful, if you're able, be wise, but above all be cautious. Now, since we can expect Suzanna to be cautious we shall begin by frightening her. We'll threaten to expose the Count's advances to her.

BARTHOLO: And where will that get us?

MARCELINE: She'll be frightened and go on refusing him. He'll exact revenge by opposing the marriage and that'll leave the way open for me to secure Figaro.

BARTHOLO: What a clever scheme! The former governess marries the wretch who robbed me of my lovely young ward…

MARCELINE: You mean…marries the charmer who thought he could be happy at my expense.

BARTHOLO: I meant…marries the thief who stole a hundred crowns from me. I shan't forget that.

MARCELINE: What a delight…

BARTHOLO: …to punish the scoundrel.

MARCELINE: And marry him, doctor, and marry him!

(Enter SUZANNA. In her hand she is holding a bonnet with a large ribbon and over her arm, a dress.)

SUZANNA: Marry him, marry him! Who do you mean? My Figaro?

MARCELINE: (*Bitterly.*) Why not? You are.

BARTHOLO: (*Laughing.*) Female logic! (*To SUZANNA.*) We were just saying what a lucky man he is.

MARCELINE: Not to mention, his Lordship!

SUZANNA: (*Curtseying.*) Your servant, señorita; do I detect a bitter note in your remarks?

MARCELINE: (*Curtseying.*) And yours, señorita. Bitterness? Surely a generous nobleman has the right to share in the joy that he procures for his servants?

SUZANNA: Did you say 'procures', señorita?

MARCELINE: Yes, señorita, 'procures'.

SUZANNA: Your jealousy is as powerful as your hold over Figaro is feeble.

MARCELINE: I'd have a stronger grip if I employed your methods.

SUZANNA: Not easy for a Lady of your years.

MARCELINE: You're no spring chicken yourself!

BARTHOLO: (*Drawing MARCELINE away.*) Farewell, Figaro's fair fiancée.

MARCELINE: (*Curtseying.*) And the Count's clandestine consort.

SUZANNA: (*Curtseying.*) Who holds you in the highest regard, señorita.

MARCELINE: (*Curtseying.*) Such a pretty young lady.

SUZANNA: (*Curtseying.*) Yes, by comparison.

MARCELINE: (*Curtseying.*) And so respectable.

SUZANNA: (*Curtseying.*) Respectability's for old maids.

MARCELINE: (*Outraged.*) Old maids! Old maids!

BARTHOLO: (*Stopping her.*) Marceline!

MARCELINE: Let's go doctor or I won't answer for my actions. (*Curtseying.*) Good day señorita.

(*BARTHOLO and MARCELINE exit.*)

SUZANNA: Good riddance. You senile schoolmarm! Just because you've made my mistress' life hell as her governess, doesn't mean to say you can rule the entire chateau. (*Throwing the dress on the chair.*) Now I've forgotten what I came in for.

(*Enter CHERUBINO running.*)

CHERUBINO: Ah Suzie! I've been waiting to try to get you on your own. I am lost! You're getting married and I'm going away!

SUZANNA: Why is his Lordship's favourite page running away because of *my* marriage?

CHERUBINO: He's sending me away, Suzanna!

SUZANNA: Have you disgraced yourself again?

CHERUBINO: He caught me with your cousin Fanchette yesterday evening. I was rehearsing her. She's playing the part of the virgin in the wedding masque. He went into a fury when he found me. 'Get out' he said to me 'you little…' I daren't repeat the word he used in front of a lady. 'Get out and tomorrow you go.' If her Ladyship can't

persuade him, it's all over, Suzanna, and
I shall never have the bliss of seeing you again.

SUZANNA: Oh it's my turn now, is it? What's happened to
her Ladyship?

CHERUBINO: She's so noble and beautiful, Suzie; but she's
my godmother and she's unapproachable.

SUZANNA: What you mean is that I am not, and that you
can try it on with me!

CHERUBINO: You know I wouldn't, temptress. But you are
so lucky! You see her every minute of the day. You talk to
her, help her put her clothes on in the mornings, undress
her at night hook by hook. Oh Suzie, what
I wouldn't give…! What's that?

SUZANNA: (*Teasingly.*) Oh! The charmed ribbon that binds
her locks and the enchanted nightcap that holds her hair in
place at night.

CHERUBINO: (*Animatedly.*) Her ribbon! Oh give it to me,
my darling!

SUZANNA: (*Holding the ribbon beyond his reach.*) Oh no! And
what do you mean, my darling! Don't get over-familiar,
you snotty-nosed brat!

(*CHERUBINO snatches the ribbon.*)

Hey, give me that back!

CHERUBINO: (*Dodging behind the armchair.*) Tell her it's torn.
Damaged. Better still, tell her it's lost. Make something up.

SUZANNA: (*Chasing him round the chair.*) In a couple of years
you're going to grow into a real devil. Now come on, give
me back that ribbon (*She tries to snatch it.*)

CHERUBINO: (*Pulling a book out of his pocket.*) Please, please
Suzie, just let me keep it. I'll give you this song
I wrote in exchange. Oh Suzie, when the memory of your
beautiful mistress makes me sad, the thought of you will
console me!

SUZANNA: (*Snatching the book.*) Console you? Who do you think you're talking to? Fanchette! You get caught with her; you pine for her Ladyship; and then you try it on with me.

CHERUBINO: You're right! I don't know what's come over me! If I so much as see a woman, my stomach turns to jelly and my heart races. The urge to say 'I love you' has become so intense that I say it to myself, to your mistress, to you, to the trees, to the clouds, to the wind that blows my soft words away to the heavens. Yesterday I came across Marceline…

SUZANNA: (*Laughing.*) That bad!

CHERUBINO: Why not? She's a woman, a maiden, a virgin, a spinster. What beautiful words. So soft, so fascinating!

SUZANNA: He's going crazy!

CHERUBINO: That's not kind! Fanchette is much nicer than you. At least she listens to me!

SUZANNA: More's the pity! Now you listen to me, young man! (*She tries to snatch the ribbon back.*)

CHERUBINO: (*Dodging her.*) Over my dead body, and if that's not enough what about a kiss?

SUZANNA: (*Dodging him.*) A slap more likely. I'll report you to my mistress; and tell his Lordship: he's right to send you back to your family. Making love to her Ladyship and trying to kiss me.

(*The COUNT enters.*)

CHERUBINO: (*Seeing the COUNT come in he throws himself behind the chair in terror.*) I've had it!

SUZANNA: What's the matter? (*Seeing the COUNT.*) Oh! (*She moves to the chair and tries to hide CHERUBINO.*)

COUNT: You're over-excited, Suzie! Talking to yourself. Red in the face. Your little bosom heaving. It's understandable, of course, on such a day.

SUZANNA: (*Worried.*) What do you want, sir? If you were found in here with me…

COUNT: That would be awkward, I agree. But you know my feelings for you. Bazile has told you of my love. All I want is one brief moment to tell you what I have in mind. Listen to me! (*He sits in the armchair.*)

SUZANNA: I won't hear a word.

COUNT: (*Taking her hand.*) You know that the King has appointed me his ambassador in London. I am going to take Figaro with me: I'm giving him an excellent job and as the wife's place is with her husband…

SUZANNA: May I say something?

COUNT: Go on, speak my darling; you know your influence over me.

SUZANNA: (*Frightened.*) I don't want any influence over you, sir. Please leave me alone.

COUNT: Tell me what you wanted to say.

SUZANNA: (*Angry.*) I can't remember.

COUNT: Something about the duties of a wife, perhaps?

SUZANNA: Oh yes! When you rescued her Ladyship from the clutches of Bartholo, you married her for love. For her sake you abolished that dreadful *droit de seigneur*…

COUNT: (*Gaily.*) …which now all the girls miss so much! Oh Suzie! It was such a charming custom! If you would only meet me in the garden at dusk I would make it so worth your while…

BAZILE: (*Off.*) He's not at home, sir.

COUNT: (*Rising.*) Who's that?

SUZANNA: We mustn't be found in here together!

COUNT: Then get out!

SUZANNA: (*Worried.*) And leave you in here alone?

BAZILE: (*Off.*) His Lordship was with her Ladyship. He's out – I'll go and see.

COUNT: Nowhere to hide. Behind this chair will have to do! Get rid of him quickly.

(*SUZANNA bars his way. He pushes her gently. She recoils and manages to put herself between the COUNT and CHERUBINO. While the COUNT gets down on his hands and knees, CHERUBINO comes round from the back of the chair and throws himself onto it, kneeling and hides his head in his hands. SUZANNA throws the dress she has been carrying over him and stands in front of the chair as BAZILE enters.*)

BAZILE: Have you seen his Lordship?

SUZANNA: (*Brusquely.*) No. Why should I have done? Get out!

BAZILE: What's the matter? It's a perfectly reasonable question. Figaro's looking for him.

SUZANNA: Figaro wants to find the man who's his worst enemy after you?

COUNT: (*Aside.*) Now let's see how loyal a servant he is.

BAZILE: Does befriending a man's wife turn him into one's enemy?

SUZANNA: Not according to the disgusting principles of a libertine like you.

BAZILE: Nothing's being asked of you that you wouldn't lavish on someone else. Thanks to one little ceremony what you aren't allowed to do today you'll be positively asked to do, tomorrow.

SUZANNA: You're a disgrace!

BAZILE: Of all conventions marriage is the most ridiculous! Now what I had in mind...

SUZANNA: (*Outraged.*) ...was surely something appalling. Anyway, who gave you permission to come in here?

BAZILE: Now, now! Temper, temper! Nothing will happen that you don't want. But I don't regard Figaro as any obstacle to his Lordship's rights. What's good for Cherubino...

SUZANNA: (*Alarmed.*) Cherubino?

BAZILE: (*Imitating her.*) Cherubino the cherub! Chasing after you all the time. This morning he was sniffing around your door waiting to come in here the moment I left. Isn't that true?

SUZANNA: No it's not. Get out of my sight you vile man.

BAZILE: Just because I keep my eyes open, I'm vile, eh? Isn't it true that he's written a love song for you?

SUZANNA: (*Angry.*) Don't be ridiculous!

BAZILE: Then perhaps it was for her Ladyship instead! He can't keep his eyes off her when he's serving at table. He'd better be careful, His Lordship can be savage!

SUZANNA: (*Outraged.*) And you're despicable enough to spread dangerous rumours. He's already out of favour with his master.

BAZILE: Me! I simply repeat what everybody says.

COUNT: (*Getting up.*) And just what is everybody saying?

SUZANNA: Oh God!

BAZILE: Your Lordship!

COUNT: Bazile! Hunt the boy down and run him off the premises.

BAZILE: I shouldn't be here!

SUZANNA: O God, O God!

COUNT: She's overcome. Sit her down.

SUZANNA: I don't want to sit down. How dare you barge in like this! It's not right.

COUNT: There are two of us here, my dear. You're in no danger.

BAZILE: I'm sorry to have made a joke about the pageboy, my Lord. I was just trying to find out about her feelings for him. Deep down I…

COUNT: Give him fifty francs, a horse and send him back to his family.

BAZILE: Because of my little joke, sir?

COUNT: He's a libertine. I found him earlier today with the gardener's daughter.

BAZILE: With Fanchette?

COUNT: In her bedroom.

SUZANNA: (*Outraged.*) Where no doubt your Excellency had business of his own to conduct!

COUNT: I went there to give your drunken uncle of a gardener his orders. The door was locked. I knocked. It took a long time. Your cousin looked a bit embarrassed. I became suspicious and engaged her in conversation. While I was talking I took a look around. Behind the door there was a cupboard with a curtain in front of it.
I pulled it back bit by bit... (*He illustrates by pulling back the dress on the chair.*) ...and I saw... (*He sees the page.*) ...ah...

BAZILE: Ah ha!

COUNT: This time we get the rear view.

BAZILE: But he's always at your service!

COUNT: (*To SUZANNA.*) And at yours too, no doubt, young lady! An aperitif before marriage? No wonder you were trying so hard to get rid of us. You wanted to be on your own with my page, didn't you? As for you, young man, your behaviour's scandalous. You have so little respect for your godmother, you've already turned your attentions to her chambermaid. And she's your friend's intended! But I won't let Figaro be deceived. I love and respect him too much for that.

SUZANNA: (*Angry.*) There's no deception; Cherubino was here the whole time you were talking to me.

COUNT: (*Equally angry.*) One lie after the other. Poor Figaro! His worst enemy wouldn't wish him such bad luck.

SUZANNA: He was begging me to get her Ladyship to intercede for him. Your arrival frightened him so much he hid behind the chair.

COUNT: (*Furious.*) Another lie! I sat down in it when I came in.

CHERUBINO: And I was trembling behind it, sir.

COUNT: But I went behind it myself!

CHERUBINO: That's when I hid on the chair.

COUNT: You little snake! He was listening to every word we said!

CHERUBINO: On the contrary sir, I did everything I could so as not to hear.

COUNT: Treachery! (*To SUZANNA.*) You, señorita, will not be marrying Figaro.

BAZILE: Somebody's coming.

COUNT: (*Dragging CHERUBINO off the armchair and making him stand up.*) Let him stand there for everybody to see!

(*Enter FIGARO, the COUNTESS, FANCHETTE, SERVANTS and PEASANTS dressed in white.*)

FIGARO: (*Carrying a woman's headdress trimmed with white feathers and ribbons. To the COUNTESS.*) Only you my Lady can help us gain this favour.

COUNTESS: (*To the COUNT.*) They think I can influence my husband! And as their request is not unreasonable…

COUNT: Naturally I'll give it proper consideration.

FIGARO: (*Aside to SUZANNA.*) Back me up!

SUZANNA: (*Aside to FIGARO.*) It's pointless.

FIGARO: (*Aside to SUZANNA.*) Just try!

COUNT: (*To FIGARO.*) Well, what is it?

FIGARO: Your Excellency! We, your servants and dependents, were deeply moved when out of love for her Ladyship, you abolished that ancient and distressing privilege…

COUNT: That's all in the past. What do you want?

FIGARO: (*Cunningly.*) Your virtuous deed should be publicly acclaimed. Since today I shall be benefiting from your goodness; I want to celebrate it at my wedding.

COUNT: (*Embarrassed.*) It was a shameful practice. Common decency demanded its abolition. A Spaniard should make such conquests by gallantry not by force. I'm a Castillian nobleman not a tyrannical Goth.

FIGARO: (*Taking SUZANNA by the hand.*) This young creature's virtue is intact due to your Excellency's moral stance. In front of these witnesses, please bestow this virgin's crown on her. It's decorated with white feathers and ribbons, as a symbol of the purity of your intentions. You should incorporate this ceremony, sir, into all future weddings in the district. Let a choral paean sung in unison remind future generations of this event.

COUNT: (*Aside.*) Fiancées, poets and musicians – they're all lunatics.

FIGARO: Hip, hip hurrah for his Lordship.

ALL: Hurrah, hurrah, hurrah!

SUZANNA: (*To the COUNT.*) Accept this tribute you so deserve.

COUNT: (*Aside.*) Treacherous bitch!

FIGARO: Look at her, sir. Could you ever ask for a more comely bride to exemplify the magnitude of your sacrifice!

SUZANNA: Enough of my comeliness! Keep praising him!

COUNT: (*Aside.*) They're playing a game with me!

COUNTESS: I join my plea to theirs, my Lord. This ceremony will always be dear to my heart because it springs from the love you once had for me.

COUNT: The love I still have, my Lady! And so I submit.

ALL: Hurrah!

COUNT: (*Aside.*) I'm trapped. (*Aloud.*) I would only ask that we postpone the ceremony for a while so that its importance can be more widely promulgated. (*Aside.*) I must find Marceline at once.

FIGARO: (*To CHERUBINO.*) What's the matter with you, young monkey? Why aren't you cheering?

SUZANNA: He's in despair. The Count's banished him.

COUNTESS: Please show him some compassion, husband.

COUNT: He doesn't deserve any.

COUNTESS: But he's so young and innocent!

COUNT: Not quite as innocent as you think!

CHERUBINO: (*To the COUNT.*) I behaved thoughtlessly your Lordship, but I never, as yet, have uttered a single indiscreet word.

COUNT: (*Embarrassed.*) Alright. That's enough.

FIGARO: What does he mean?

COUNT: (*Sharply.*) I've heard enough. Everybody wants him pardoned. So I forgive him. And I'll do more than that. I'll give him a company in my regiment to command.

ALL: Hurrah!

COUNT: But on condition that he leaves to join it immediately. It's in Catalonia.

FIGARO: Tomorrow, my Lord?

COUNT: Now!

CHERUBINO: I'm on my way!

COUNT: Say goodbye to your godmother and ask for her blessing.

(*CHERUBINO goes down on one knee in front of the COUNTESS but is speechless.*)

COUNTESS: We can't even keep you one day longer, young man. So go. A new life beckons. A new role. Fulfil it worthily. Honour your patron. Don't forget this house where your youth was indulged. Now go out into the world and be obedient, brave and valiant. We shall all share in your triumphs.

(*CHERUBINO gets up.*)

COUNT: You seem overcome, Madame.

COUNTESS: Of course I am. Who knows what might happen to a young boy in such a dangerous career? Besides he's a relative and he's my godchild.

COUNT: (*Aside.*) So Bazile was right. (*Loud.*) Young man, give Suzanna a kiss. For the last time.

FIGARO: Why sir? He'll come back on leave. Give me a hug too, captain. Goodbye, Cherubino. You're off to lead a different life now. No more hanging round the ladies' quarters. No more chocolate eclairs and cream and blindman's buff. You're a soldier now. Ragged-arsed, weatherbeaten, a heavy rifle on your shoulder. Right turn! Left turn! Forward march to glory! Onwards until the bullet strikes!

SUZANNA: For heaven's sake, Figaro!

COUNTESS: What a future!

COUNT: Where's Marceline? It's odd she isn't here.

FANCHETTE: My Lord.

COUNT: Fanchette?

FANCHETTE: She went into town. As the proverb goes.

COUNT: Isn't she coming back?

BAZILE: In God's good time.

FIGARO: Never. If he's feeling kind.

FANCHETTE: Doctor Bartholo was with her.

COUNT: (*Sharply.*) The doctor's here?

BAZILE: She grabbed him as soon as he arrived.

COUNT: He couldn't have come at a better moment.

FANCHETTE: She seemed very annoyed. She was shouting at the top of her voice about cousin Figaro.

COUNT: (*Chucking her under the chin.*) Cousin...to be.

FANCHETTE: Has your Lordship forgiven us for last night?

COUNT: Goodbye, goodbye, my child. (*Aside.*) She'll succeed, I promise you. (*Loud.*) Come my Lady. Bazile, see me in my rooms.

SUZANNA: (*To FIGARO.*) You will come back won't you?

FIGARO: (*Aside to SUZANNA.*) Is he hooked?

SUZANNA: Clever boy!

(*They all go out except for FIGARO who holds back both CHERUBINO and BAZILE.*)

FIGARO: Just a moment, you two. The ceremony's agreed to so the wedding will take place. Now let's rehearse our roles. We don't want to be like actors who always perform badly when the critics turn up. Today's the one chance we've got. So let's get our parts right.

BAZILE: (*Slyly.*) Mine is more difficult than you imagine.

FIGARO: (*Making a gesture of slapping him without his seeing.*) You don't know how rewarding it'll be for you.

CHERUBINO: Have you forgotten that I've got to leave?

FIGARO: No I haven't. But wouldn't you prefer to stay?

CHERUBINO: If only I could.

FIGARO: Be clever. Don't complain about having to go. Do your packing publicly. Carry your travelling coat over your arm. Have your horse outside at the ready. Then gallop as far as the farm and come back on foot the back way. His Excellency will think you've gone for good. Just make sure you keep out of his sight. I'll talk him round when the celebrations are over.

CHERUBINO: But Fanchette doesn't know her part yet.

BAZILE: Then what the devil have you been teaching her for the last week? You've hardly left her side!

FIGARO: You've nothing to do today so give her another rehearsal.

BAZILE: Be careful, young man. Her father's already angry. He knows what the two of you have been rehearsing and he's already spanked her. You'll only get her into trouble. If you lower a bucket down the well…

FIGARO: Enough proverbs, you old pedant. Oh go on then, startle us with the wisdom of the world. What does happen when you lower a bucket down the well?

BAZILE: It gets filled of course.

FIGARO: Not bad! Not bad!

End of Act One.

ACT TWO

A sumptuously furnished bedroom with a bed in a recess and a small rostrum downstage of it. There are three doors: the main door to the room upstage right, a door to a dressing room downstage left and an upstage door to the chambermaid's room far upstage. On the opposite side of the room there is a window. SUZANNA and the COUNTESS enter from the door right.

COUNTESS: (*Throwing herself into a large armchair.*) Shut the door, Suzanna. Tell me exactly what happened.

SUZANNA: I've told you the whole truth.

COUNTESS: He wanted to seduce you?

SUZANNA: Seduce me! That's too much like hard work for the Count! He wanted to pay me for my services.

COUNTESS: And the pageboy was in the same room?

SUZANNA: In a manner of speaking. He was hiding behind the armchair. He'd come to ask me if you would intercede for him.

COUNTESS: Why didn't he come to me himself? Does he think I'd have turned him down?

SUZANNA: That's what I said. But he was so upset at the prospect of leaving and most of all of leaving you, my Lady. 'Oh Suzie,' he said, 'she's so noble and fine. But so unapproachable.'

COUNTESS: Unapproachable! But I've always protected him.

SUZANNA: Then he saw your ribbon in my hand. He grabbed it.

COUNTESS: (*Smiling.*) My ribbon?

SUZANNA: He fought like a lion when I tried to get it back. You should have seen his eyes flashing.

COUNTESS: (*Dreamily.*) What delightful foolishness! But
what about you Suzie. What did my husband say in the
end?

SUZANNA: That if I wouldn't listen to him, he'd support
Marceline.

COUNTESS: (*Getting up and fanning herself vigorously.*) He
doesn't love me at all.

SUZANNA: Then why is he so jealous?

COUNTESS: He's a husband. They're all the same! Driven
by pride! I showed him too much affection. I wearied him
with my love. That's my only fault. But I shan't let your
refusing him stand in the way of your marriage to Figaro.
He's the only man who can help us. Is he coming?

SUZANNA: As soon as the hunt moves off.

COUNTESS: Open the garden window, will you. It's hot in
here.

SUZANNA: That's because you're pacing up and down, My
Lady.

COUNTESS: (*Deep in thought.*) Chasing other women when
I've been so faithful. Men!

SUZANNA: (*At the window.*) There goes his Lordship now.

COUNTESS: Then we've got time. (*She sits.*) Was that
someone knocking, Suzie?

SUZANNA: (*Running to the door.*) My Figaro!

(*Enter FIGARO.*)

Figaro, Her Ladyship is desperate to see you.

FIGARO: And you're not, Suzie? (*To the COUNTESS.*) There's
no need to worry. He's just up to his usual tricks. He finds
a young woman attractive and so he tries to make her his
mistress. What could be more normal?

SUZANNA: Normal?

FIGARO: Then because my fiancée won't accept him, he
supports Marceline's cause instead. What's unusual about

that? He's only getting his own back. You thwart his plans so he thwarts yours. It's exactly what we're going to do.

COUNTESS: How can you treat our misfortune so lightly?

FIGARO: What do you mean, My Lady?

COUNTESS: Don't our problems depress you?

FIGARO: Solving them is the antidote! We shall have to adopt the Count's own method. Temper his ardour for what belongs to us by undermining his confidence in what belongs to him.

COUNTESS: How?

FIGARO: I've already done it! A little rumour about her Ladyship in one ear…

COUNTESS: About me? You must be mad!

FIGARO: I'm not – but he soon will be.

COUNTESS: But he's such a jealous man!

FIGARO: So much the better. Now, I've sent an anonymous letter to Bazile. It warns his Lordship that a gallant is going to seek you out at the ball tonight.

COUNTESS: Figaro, I am a woman of honour.

FIGARO: There are very few women with whom I'd take the risk, my Lady. Just in case it was true!

COUNTESS: Thank you for your confidence.

FIGARO: Instead of chasing my wife, he'll be running around cursing his own! Should he look here? Should he hunt there? Over the fields he goes. Chasing this hare, then that one. And nothing can help him. The hour of the wedding approaches and he's not done anything to stop it. And once he's in your presence My Lady, he'd never dare to.

SUZANNA: But Marceline would!

FIGARO: I know. She worries me. Now, send word to his Lordship that you'll meet him in the garden at dusk.

SUZANNA: You still think that'll work?

FIGARO: People who don't try, never succeed.

SUZANNA: Alright, I'll give it a go.

COUNTESS: You are not going to let her go through with it, surely?

FIGARO: Of course not. I'll dress somebody else in her clothes. When we spring the ambush he won't be able to deny that it was really Suzie he wanted to meet.

SUZANNA: Who's going to play me?

FIGARO: Cherubino.

COUNTESS: But he's already left.

FIGARO: I know differently. Now leave it all to me!

SUZANNA: There's no better plotter than Figaro.

FIGARO: Two, three, four schemes at a time. Criss-crossed and tangled. I love complexity. I should have been a politician!

SUZANNA: They say it's a difficult calling.

FIGARO: Take, take and take. That's their secret in three words!

SUZANNA: Your self-confidence is inspiring.

FIGARO: Now, while his Lordship's away I'll send Cherubino to you. Dress him and arrange his hair. I'll teach him what to do and then, let's watch his Lordship dance! (*He exits.*)

COUNTESS: (*With her powder compact in hand.*) Good heavens, Suzie, just look at me! And Cherubino is coming!

SUZANNA: You are not going to let him off, are you?

COUNTESS: Let him off! Just you see how I scold him!

SUZANNA: Get him to sing the love song he wrote for you. (*She takes the book out of her pocket.*)

COUNTESS: My hair is all over the place.

SUZANNA: (*Laughing.*) If I just put these two curls back in place, you'll scold him all the better!

(*CHERUBINO enters looking disconsolate.*)

You may come in, captain.

CHERUBINO: (*Trembling.*) Horrible word! It reminds me that I must leave here…must leave my godmother…who has been so kind…

SUZANNA: …and so beautiful!

CHERUBINO: (*Sighing.*) Oh yes!

SUZANNA: (*Imitating.*) Oh yes! You poor young thing with your crocodile tears. Come on little nightingale, sing your song for her Ladyship.

COUNTESS: Who is the song for, may I ask?

SUZANNA: He's blushing. Anybody'd think he'd got wind.

CHERUBINO: Is it wrong to be in love?

SUZANNA: (*Threatening him with her fist.*) I'll tell her everything, you wretch!

COUNTESS: I'm ready. Is he going to sing?

CHERUBINO: I am a bag of nerves, your Ladyship.

SUZANNA: Come on, I'll accompany you.

COUNTESS: Take my guitar.

(*The COUNTESS is sitting in the armchair holding the book of ballads to follow the words. SUZANNA is behind the armchair, looking over her shoulder to follow the music. The page faces the COUNTESS, eyes downcast.*)

CHERUBINO: Twas where a rill was breaking,
My heart my heart is aching
For her I was forsaking
I felt the tears flow
I felt the tears flow
My trusty danger taking
My heart my heart is aching
I carved with a hand a quaking her name upon a tree
The Queen then pity taking
My heart my heart is aching
Quoth 'Page what ails thee making thee so sadly so to
                                                    sigh?'
'Queen though the camp is waking'
My heart my heart is aching

The lady I'm forsaking I'll love until I die
I'll love until I die.

COUNTESS: Innocent…and yet strangely moving.

SUZANNA: Oh please! Now captain, to add pleasure to the evening we want to see if you'll fit into one of my dresses.

COUNTESS: I am afraid he's too big.

SUZANNA: (*Measuring herself against him.*) He's the right height. Let's have his coat off first. (*She takes it off him.*)

COUNTESS: What if someone comes in?

SUZANNA: We're not doing anything wrong but I'll lock the door just in case. I want to see what we can do with his hair.

COUNTESS: There's a wig of mine on the dressing table.

(*SUZANNA goes into the dressing room.*)

The Count shouldn't know you're still in the chateau until just before the party. We'll tell him that you had to wait for your commission papers.

CHERUBINO: (*Showing her.*) But I've already got it. Bazile gave it me.

COUNTESS: What? They don't waste time. (*Reading it.*) They left in such a hurry they've forgotten the seal. (*She gives it back to him.*)

(*SUZANNA re-enters with a large wig.*)

SUZANNA: (*Sitting next to the COUNTESS.*) This one should do. (*She sings with pins in her mouth.*)

Turn your face to mine,
Let my lips touch thine…

(*CHERUBINO gets on his knees as she pins the hair on him.*)

Doesn't he look lovely, my Lady?

COUNTESS: Let a bit more hair hang over the collar. It's more feminine.

SUZANNA: (*Arranging it.*) There! He makes a lovely girl! I'm almost jealous! (*Chucking CHERUBINO's chin.*) Wouldn't you like to be as pretty?

COUNTESS: Silly girl! Pull back his sleeves so that the cuffs stick out more. (*She pushes back a sleeve revealing her ribbon.*) What's this?

SUZANNA: It's the one of yours I was telling you about. If his Lordship hadn't blundered into the room I'd have got it back from him. I'm almost as strong as he is.

COUNTESS: (*Undoing it.*) There's blood on it.

CHERUBINO: My horse bit me this morning as I was preparing to leave.

COUNTESS: Wouldn't a bandage have been better?

SUZANNA: Than a stolen ribbon? Oh no! Eh Cherubino? But just look at how white his arm is. It's a girl's arm. Even whiter than mine. Just look my Lady!

COUNTESS: (*Icily.*) Wouldn't you be better employed fetching me some lint for his wound? There's some in my dressing room.

(*SUZANNA, laughing, pushes CHERUBINO over onto the floor. She goes into the dressing room.*

The COUNTESS pauses while admiring her ribbon. CHERUBINO meanwhile admires her.)

I'm very fond it. The colour suits me. I would have been upset to lose it.

SUZANNA: (*Re-entering with lint and scissors.*) How are you going to bind it to his arm?

COUNTESS: While you're looking for dresses for him, take the ribbon out of another hat.

(*SUZANNA goes off to her own room taking CHERUBINO's coat with her.*)

CHERUBINO: The one I had on would have healed me in no time at all.

COUNTESS: How? (*Showing him the lint.*) This'll be much better.

CHERUBINO: The one I had on had touched the skin of a certain…

COUNTESS: …unknown person? Do you think it's acquired curative powers? Well! I must try it on one of my women. I'll keep it until one of them cuts themselves.

CHERUBINO: The ribbon will be here and I'll be far away.

COUNTESS: You'll come back.

CHERUBINO: I am so miserable!

COUNTESS: (*Moved.*) He's crying. It's all Figaro's fault. Forced marches. Bullets striking their targets!

CHERUBINO: I wish that hour had come! If I were dying now, my lips might dare to…

COUNTESS: (*Comforting him.*) Hush! Hush! What nonsense!
(*There is a knock at the door.*)
Who's that?

COUNT: (*Off.*) Why have you locked the door?

COUNTESS: It's my husband! And you're half-undressed! Alone with me! And by now he'll have had the letter. He'll be mad with jealousy.

COUNT: (*Off.*) Are you going to open up?

COUNTESS: Yes, of course. But I'm on my own.

COUNT: (*Off.*) Then who are you talking to?

COUNTESS: To…to…to…to you, of course.

CHERUBINO: (*Aside.*) After what went on yesterday… and this morning, he'll kill me on the spot. (*He runs to the dressing room and pulls the door shut behind him.*)

COUNTESS: How could we be so stupid! (*She runs to the main door with the key and unlocks it.*)

COUNT: (*Enters.*) You don't normally lock yourself in!

COUNTESS: I was… I was…sewing! Yes I was sewing with Suzie; she's just gone through to her own room.

COUNT: You look agitated.

COUNTESS: Not surprising…we were talking about you…

COUNT: Talking about me, were you? Well I'm beside myself! I was just mounting my horse when somebody put a letter into my hand. I don't believe a word of what it says of course but it's upset me.

COUNTESS: What does it say?

COUNT: It warns me that during the course of the day, a man, whom I believe to be far away from here, is going to try to gain access to you.

COUNTESS: He'll have to be resourceful. I don't intend to leave my room all day.

COUNT: Not even for Suzanna's wedding this afternoon?

COUNTESS: Not even for that. I don't feel at all well.

COUNT: Lucky the doctor's here.

(*There is a noise off in the dressing room.*)

What's that noise?

COUNTESS: What noise?

COUNT: In there.

COUNTESS: I didn't hear anything.

COUNT: Are you deaf?

COUNTESS: I must have been miles away.

COUNT: There's somebody in there.

COUNTESS: And who do you think it could be? Who would want to hide in my dressing room?

COUNT: How should I know!

COUNTESS: It must be Suzanna rummaging around.

COUNT: I thought you said she was in her room.

COUNTESS: She certainly went out somewhere. I can't remember which door she went through.

COUNT: If it's Suzanna, why are you blushing?

COUNTESS: Why should I blush over my chambermaid?

COUNT: I don't know. But your cheeks are very red!

COUNTESS: It's not me whose cheeks redden at the thought of her!

COUNT: (*Angry.*) I don't know what you mean! But I want her here right now.

COUNTESS: Don't I know it! Anyway your suspicions are groundless…

(*Enter SUZANNA from her room.*)

COUNT: Then I can dispose of them easily. (*Speaking to the dressing room door.*) Come out here, Suzanna. That's an order.

(*SUZANNA stops upstage near the alcove.*)

COUNTESS: She's practically naked, my Lord. Do you think it's appropriate behaviour to break in here and disturb us like this? She's trying on some clothes I gave her as a wedding present. She rushed in there when she heard your voice.

COUNT: If she's scared of showing herself, she might at least speak to me. (*To the door.*) Say something Suzanna. Are you in there?

(*SUZANNA hides in the alcove.*)

COUNTESS: I forbid you to answer, Suzie. (*To the COUNT.*) You're acting like a despot.

COUNT: Well if she won't talk to me, I'll go in and see her, naked or not.

COUNTESS: (*Inserting herself between the COUNT and the door.*) This is my room. The one place where I give the orders.

COUNT: That won't prevent me from finding out who this mysterious Suzanna really is. To ask you for the key would be pointless so I'll have the door broken down. (*Calling for help.*) Hello there!

COUNTESS: Go on then! Call your servants! Create a public scandal. Make us the laughing stock of the chateau just for a silly suspicion!

COUNT: Alright, I'll do it. I'll go and get some tools. But just so everything remains as it is, you come with me. Do it quietly and you won't attract the attention of the scandalmongers whom you appear to hate so much. I assume you won't refuse.

COUNTESS: (*Worried.*) How could I refuse you anything, my Lord.

COUNT: I mustn't forget to lock the door that leads to the maid's quarters. (*He locks the upstage door.*)

COUNTESS: (*Aside.*) Oh God! He's so thorough!

COUNT: Now that we're all locked up, you may take my arm. And as for Suzanna in the dressing room, she'll have the good grace to wait for my return; I don't think she'll come to any harm!

COUNTESS: This is all very unpleasant!

(*They exit, the COUNT locking the door behind him.*)

SUZANNA: (*Coming out of the alcove she runs to the dressing room door and addresses her remarks through the keyhole.*) Quick! Cherubino! Open up! Get out of there!

CHERUBINO: (*Entering.*) Suzie! This is terrible!

SUZANNA: You must leave right now. There's not a moment to lose.

CHERUBINO: But how do I get out of here?

SUZANNA: I don't know. Just go.

CHERUBINO: But there isn't a way out.

SUZANNA: After that scene, he'll cut you up into little pieces and that'll be the end of us all. Run and tell Figaro…

CHERUBINO: (*Running to the window.*) Is this window too high?

SUZANNA: Impossible! We're on the first floor. Oh my poor mistress! And my wedding! Oh God!

CHERUBINO: (*Opening the window.*) There's a bed of melons down there. I might damage one or two of them. But I think I can do it.

SUZANNA: You'll kill yourself!

CHERUBINO: (*Melodramatically.*) Into the abyss I go Suzie! Rather than a hair of her head be harmed! This kiss will bring me luck! (*He kisses her and takes a running jump out of the window.*)

SUZANNA: (*She screams.*) Oh! (*She falls into a chair. Then slowly and miserably goes to the window and looks out.*) He's done it! He's nearly out of sight already. Handsome and athletic! He'll always have women after him! Now, your Lordship, (*She goes into the dressing room.*) I'm ready for you. Break the door down if you want. (*She locks the door.*)

(*The COUNT and the COUNTESS re-enter.*)

COUNT: (*He is holding a pair of pincers.*) Good! Just as I left it! Before I break down this door, my Lady, please consider the consequences and unlock it for me?

COUNTESS: Why are you trying to wreck our marriage? If it were love that had driven you into such frenzy I could forgive you. But for a man of honour to indulge in such offensive behaviour out of mere vanity...!

COUNT: Love or vanity, either you open this door or I...

COUNTESS: Very well, my Lord. You *will* see. But first I want you to listen calmly to my explanation.

COUNT: You mean it isn't Suzanna.

COUNTESS: Not exactly. It's someone...someone whom you've no reason to mistrust...someone with whom I was planning a joke...an innocent prank for this evening's party...and I swear...

COUNT: What?

COUNTESS: That neither of us intended to cause you offence.

COUNT: This other person? It wouldn't be a man, by any chance?

COUNTESS: A boy, my Lord.

COUNT: Who do you mean?

COUNTESS: I daren't tell you.

COUNT: (*Furiously.*) I'll kill him.

COUNTESS: Good God!

COUNT: His name!

COUNTESS: …Cherubino.

COUNT: Everywhere I turn I come across that wretched page.

COUNTESS: My Lord.

COUNT: It's all true, the letter. He's the secret paramour.

COUNTESS: My Lord, please don't think…

COUNT: (*To the COUNTESS.*) Open up, My Lady! Now I understand everything. Why you were so moved when he left this morning. Why he didn't go when I commanded him and why you lied about Suzanna being in there. And why were you so secretive about him if you've got nothing to hide?

COUNTESS: He was frightened.

COUNT: (*Shouting at the door.*) Come out, you scoundrel!

COUNTESS: (*Pushing him away from the door.*) Don't be so angry! I'm frightened for the boy's safety. Now when you see him, don't let his state of undress worry you.

COUNT: Undress!

COUNTESS: Yes, he was trying out a disguise for this evening with my clothes…

COUNT: Out of my way.

COUNTESS: My Lord! Please spare the boy! I could never forgive myself for having caused...

COUNT: Get up! How dare you plead to me for another man.

COUNTESS: But in the name of your love for me...

COUNT: My love! You loose woman!

COUNTESS: (*Giving him the key.*) Promise me that you'll let him go free. Unharmed!

COUNT: I'm not listening.

COUNTESS: (*Throwing herself into the chair.*) Oh God! He's done for!

COUNT: (*Opening the door.*) Silence! Suzanna!

SUZANNA: (*Enters laughing.*) 'I'll kill him! I'll kill him.' Go on then! Kill the naughty pageboy.

COUNT: (*Aside.*) Is this an April Fool? (*Looking at the astonished COUNTESS.*) Why are you acting so surprised? Perhaps there's someone else in there. (*He goes into the dressing room.*)

SUZANNA: (*Aside to the COUNTESS.*) Pull yourself together, my Lady. He's far away by now. He jumped out of the window.

COUNTESS: I can't take any more of this!

COUNT: (*Re-entering.*) Nobody! I was wrong! You're quite an actress.

SUZANNA: What about me?

COUNT: You keep out of it.

(*The COUNTESS puts her handkerchief to her mouth trying to regain her composure. She remains silent.*)

So you were joking, were you?

COUNTESS: (*Recovering a little.*) Why shouldn't I?

COUNT: A pretty poor joke! What was its purpose?

COUNTESS: You expect me to show sympathy for your madness?

COUNT: Madness? My honour was at stake.

COUNTESS: (*Gradually becoming more assured.*) Do you think I married you to be perpetually neglected and made the object of completely unjustified jealousy?

COUNT: That's a little harsh!

SUZANNA: Her Ladyship could have let you call the servants.

COUNT: You're right. I should be ashamed of myself. Forgive me, I am somewhat confused!

COUNTESS: What you've committed is an outrage! I shall have no alternative but to enter a convent. I should have done it long ago.

COUNT: Rosine!

COUNTESS: I am not the same Rosine you courted! I am the poor Countess Almaviva, a sadly neglected woman whom you no longer love.

SUZANNA: My Lady.

COUNT: (*Begging.*) Have pity on me.

COUNTESS: You never showed me any.

COUNT: It was the letter. It made my blood boil.

COUNTESS: I didn't ask him to write it.

COUNT: Who?

COUNTESS: That idiot, Figaro…

COUNT: Him?

COUNTESS: He sent it to Bazile.

COUNT: Who told me he'd got it from a peasant. The double-crossing singing tutor! He'll pay for this!

COUNTESS: You seek my pardon yet you won't extend it to others. Men! Now listen, if I agree to forgive you for the mistake that this letter has caused it's only on condition that the amnesty is universal.

COUNT: With all my heart, Countess. But how can I atone for such a humiliating blunder?

COUNTESS: (*Getting up.*) There was error on both sides.

COUNT: Please don't blame yourself! But I still don't understand how women can so quickly and convincingly act a part. You were blushing, weeping, your face was drawn – in fact, it still is.

COUNTESS: I was blushing because of your imputations. Can't men tell the difference between the indignation of an honest woman and the embarrassment of a guilty one?

COUNT: (*Smiling.*) Between finding a half-naked pageboy and…

COUNTESS: (*Indicating SUZANNA.*) …and discovering the young lady you see before you. Aren't you pleased to have found her rather than the page? You don't normally object.

COUNT: (*Laughing.*) But your entreaties and tears were so convincing…

COUNTESS: This is no laughing matter.

COUNT: We men think we know something about diplomacy. But we're babes in arms compared with you women.

COUNTESS: You've driven us to it.

COUNT: Tell me again that you forgive me.

COUNTESS: Did I say that, Suzie?

SUZANNA: Not that I heard, My Lady.

COUNT: Then let the word pass your lips now.

COUNTESS: Do you deserve it, ungrateful man?

COUNT: My repentance does.

SUZANNA: Imagining there was a man in her Ladyship's dressing room!

COUNT: I've been severely punished for it!

SUZANNA: Doubting her when she said it was her chambermaid!

COUNT: Are you made of stone, Rosine?

COUNTESS: How frail we are, Suzie! I am going to set you such a poor example! (*Giving the COUNT her hand.*) Don't believe in the wrath of women.

SUZANNA: We always give in, in the end!

(*The COUNT kisses the COUNTESS' hand ardently. FIGARO enters out of breath.*)

FIGARO: They said your Ladyship was unwell. I ran all the way here…but you're fine.

COUNT: You're very attentive!

FIGARO: It's my duty, Sir. But as her Ladyship's alright and the youngsters are waiting with their fiddles and bagpipes, would you mind if my bride accompanied me down below?

COUNT: Who'll look after the Countess?

FIGARO: Look after her? She's not ill.

COUNT: And what about the certain person who's coming to visit her?

FIGARO: Which certain person?

COUNT: The one in the letter you sent to Bazile.

FIGARO: Letter?

COUNT: If I didn't know you were lying, you scoundrel, your face would give you away.

FIGARO: It's not me who's lying, it's my face.

SUZANNA: Sweetheart! No more fibbing! We've told him everything.

FIGARO: Everything?

SUZANNA: How you wrote the letter to make him think that the pageboy was in the dressing room, when all the time it was me.

COUNT: What have you got to say for yourself?

COUNTESS: Don't hide anything from him Figaro. The game is up.

FIGARO: (*Trying to guess what she means.*) The game…is
…up?

COUNT: The joke's over. Now, what have you got to say?

FIGARO: That I wish my wedding was over too, Sir. If you'd
give the order for it to begin.

COUNT: Then you admit the letter?

FIGARO: If that's what her Ladyship wants, and it's what
Suzie wants, and it's what you want then I suppose it's
what I want as well. But if I were in your shoes, my Lord, I
wouldn't believe a word we said.

COUNT: You're still lying! Against all the evidence. You're
beginning to irritate me.

COUNTESS: (*Laughing.*) Why do you suddenly expect him to
tell the truth after all these years?

FIGARO: (*Aside to SUZANNA.*) I've warned him not to believe
us. What else can an honest man do.

SUZANNA: (*Aside.*) Have you seen the pageboy?

FIGARO: (*Aside.*) He's still in shock.

SUZANNA: (*Aside.*) Poor thing!

COUNTESS: Come my Lord! They're dying with impatience.
They want to get married. Let's go down so the ceremony
can begin.

COUNT: (*Aside.*) Where's Marceline? (*Loud.*) I need a change
of clothes.

COUNTESS: Change for the servants! Have I done so?

(*Enter ANTONIO, half-drunk. He is holding a broken flowerpot
of wallflowers.*)

ANTONIO: My Lord! My Lord!

COUNT: What do you want, Antonio?

ANTONIO: Bars on the windows. At least on those that look
onto my flowerbeds. They throw all sorts of junk onto
them and just now they threw a man.

COUNT: From this window?

ANTONIO: Right on to my melons. Look what he's done to my wallflowers.

SUZANNA: (*Aside to FIGARO.*) Watch out, Figaro!

FIGARO: My Lord, he's been drinking all morning.

ANTONIO: You're wrong! I'm still hungover from yesterday.

COUNT: Where is this man? Where is he?

ANTONIO: Where is he?

COUNT: Yes.

ANTONIO: That's what I want to know. Somebody should look for him. I'm the person who looks after your Lordship's garden. When a man falls into it, it's my reputation that's called into question.

SUZANNA: (*Aside to FIGARO.*) Change the subject!

FIGARO: Still drinking then?

ANTONIO: I'd go mad without a drink.

COUNTESS: But do you need to drink all the time?

ANTONIO: Drinking when you're not thirsty and copulating whenever you feel like it, is the difference between men and beasts.

COUNT: Tell me where the man went or I'll have you dismissed.

ANTONIO: You wouldn't do that?

COUNT: Why not?

ANTONIO: (*Touching his forehead.*) If you haven't got enough up here to know when to keep a good servant, I'm not so daft as to give up a good master.

COUNT: (*Shaking him angrily.*) You said that somebody threw a man out of this window?

ANTONIO: Yes, your Lordship. Just now. He was in a white jacket – and he sprinted off.

COUNT: And then?

ANTONIO: I wanted to go after him but I ran into the railings and gave myself such a whack that I couldn't move a muscle.

COUNT: But you'd recognise this man again?

ANTONIO: I would…if I'd have had a good look that is!

SUZANNA: (*Aside to FIGARO.*) He doesn't know who it was.

FIGARO: What a song and dance about a flowerpot! How much do I owe you for your wallflowers, you miserable old drunkard? There's no point in looking for anyone else, my Lord. I was the one who jumped.

COUNT: You!

ANTONIO: 'Miserable old drunkard'! You've grown a bit since your jump. You were a good deal shorter and thinner then.

FIGARO: I was crouching.

ANTONIO: I think the man who jumped was more like that little runt of a pageboy.

COUNT: Do you mean Cherubino?

FIGARO: Yes he rode all the way back here at breakneck speed on horseback from the outskirts of Seville!

ANTONIO: I didn't see a horse. He wasn't on it. Not when he jumped anyway. I'd have said so.

COUNT: God give me patience!

FIGARO: I was in the bedroom in my white jacket. It was very hot! I was waiting for Suzanna when I heard your Lordship in a fury. I panicked about the letter, jumped out of the window onto the flowerbed and twisted my ankle in the process. (*He rubs his foot.*)

ANTONIO: Then I'd better let you have this scroll that fell out of your pocket.

COUNT: Give it to me. (*He seizes it and unrolls it.*)

FIGARO: (*Aside.*) That's done it.

COUNT: (*To FIGARO.*) I don't suppose your attack of panic made you forget the contents of this paper nor how it came to be in your pocket?

FIGARO: (*Embarrassed, he searches in his pocket and pulls out various papers.*) Of course not. But I do have a lot of papers. I have so many letters to reply to. (*He looks at one of them.*) This one's a four-page letter from Marceline. This is a request from a poor poacher in jail. No that's this one. Here's an inventory of the furniture in the lodge, and here…

(*The COUNT unrolls the scroll again.*)

COUNTESS: (*Aside to SUZANNA.*) It's the commission.

SUZANNA: (*Aside to FIGARO.*) It's his officer's commission.

COUNT: (*Refolding the scroll.*) Well Figaro the famous improviser can't you guess what it is?

ANTONIO: (*To FIGARO.*) His Lordship says, can't you guess?

FIGARO: You're breathing in my face.

COUNT: You can't remember what's in it then?

FIGARO: Oh God! Oh God! Oh God! Oh God! It must be the poor boy's commission. He gave it me for safekeeping and I forgot to give it him back. What a fool I am! What'll he do without it? I must go after him and…

COUNT: Why did he give it you?

FIGARO: He wanted me…to add something to it.

COUNT: It looks all right to me.

COUNTESS: (*Aside to SUZANNA.*) The seal!

SUZANNA: (*Aside to FIGARO.*) The seal's missing.

COUNT: (*To FIGARO.*) There's nothing missing.

FIGARO: There was definitely something missing, he said. Isn't it usual…

COUNT: Usual?

FIGARO: To apply your seal to it with its coat of arms.

COUNT: (*Crumpling up the paper in anger.*) I'm obviously not meant to get to the bottom of this. (*Aside.*) Figaro's behind it all. I want my revenge! (*He makes to go.*)

FIGARO: (*Stopping him.*) You're not going, are you my Lord? Won't you give the order for my marriage to take place before you leave?

(*Enter MARCELINE, BAZILE, BARTHOLO, SUNBURN and others of the COUNT's household and retinue.*)

MARCELINE: Give no such order, my Lord! I demand justice. This man is legally engaged to me by signed contract.

COUNT: (*Aside.*) At last!

(*The COUNTESS sits down. SUZANNA is behind her.*)

Explain, Marceline.

MARCELINE: He's contracted to me in marriage.

FIGARO: An IOU for money lent, that's all.

MARCELINE: Lent on condition that he'd marry me. You are a nobleman, the principal judge of this province…

COUNT: Present your case to the tribunal. There I dispense justice to all comers.

BAZILE: (*Indicating MARCELINE.*) In that case, your Lordship will permit me to press my claim over Marceline!

COUNT: (*Aside.*) The postman!

FIGARO: Another idiot!

COUNT: Your claim! Your claim indeed! How dare you talk of claims in front of me, you ass!

ANTONIO: Got him in one, your Lordship!

COUNT: Everything is suspended until we have examined your case, Marceline. That'll take place in public in the great hall. Bazile, my trusted and faithful agent! Go to town and summon the magistrates.

BAZILE: For her case?

COUNT: And you can fetch the peasant who wrote the letter.

BAZILE: Do I know him?

COUNT: Are you refusing?

BAZILE: I didn't come to this chateau to run errands.

COUNT: Then why did you come?

BAZILE: To play the village organ, show her Ladyship how to play the harpsichord, tutor her ladies in the art of singing and teach the pageboys the mandolin. But my main function is to entertain your Lordship's guests on my guitar whenever you command me to do so. I'm an artist not an errand boy.

SUNBURN: I'll go my Lord, if it please you.

COUNT: What's your name and what do you do?

SUNBURN: I'm Sunburn, your Lordship's herdboy. I look after the goats but I've come for the fireworks today. As my herd's got a day off I can find all those legal people you want fetched.

COUNT: It's a pleasure to see such enthusiasm. Off you go! (*To BAZILE.*) And you can go with him. Play the guitar, sing and entertain him on the way. Treat him as though he were a guest of mine.

SUNBURN: What me! Am I a guest?

BAZILE: Go with him and play the guitar!

COUNT: And sing as well! That's your job. Go on, or I'll have you dismissed. (*Exits.*)

BAZILE: (*Aside.*) I'll grin and bear it. But I'll make sure of my own marriage to Marceline instead of helping them with theirs. (*To FIGARO.*) Don't conclude anything till I get back, will you? (*He goes to fetch his guitar from the armchair.*)

FIGARO: (*Follows BAZILE.*) Conclude? No fear of that even if you were never to return. You lot don't look as though you're in singing mood. Shall I start you off? Here we go. Doh-la-doh. A song for my bride. (*He leads the assembled company in a seguidilla.*)

(BAZILE accompanies FIGARO.)

Wisdom not wealth
That's my Suzanna
Anne-anne-anne-anne
Anne-anne-anne-anne
Kindness and love
That's my Suzie
Ette-ette-ette-ette
Ette-ette-ette-ette

(The procession moves off singing.)

COUNTESS: What a mess that man of yours got me into with his letter.

SUZANNA: You should have seen your face when I came back into the room! It was drained of all colour, like a white cloud. Then it began to get redder, and redder and redder.

COUNTESS: Did he really jump out of the window?

SUZANNA: Without hesitating. He flew like a bumble-bee.

COUNTESS: As for that drunken gardener! I was beside myself. I couldn't think of what to say.

SUZANNA: On the contrary My Lady: you made me see how effortlessly ladies of distinction can lie.

COUNTESS: You think the Count was taken in? What if he finds the pageboy's still in the chateau?

SUZANNA: I'll make sure he has a good hiding place.

COUNTESS: He must get away from here. After what's happened he can't go to the garden in your place.

SUZANNA: Well, I'm certainly not going. And my marriage has been postponed again.

COUNTESS: Just a moment. Instead of substituting somebody else, why don't I make the rendezvous myself?

SUZANNA: You, my Lady?

COUNTESS: Nobody's put at risk. The Count won't be able to deny anything that takes place. I'll punish his jealousy and prove his infidelity. We've done well so far let's try again. Let him know that you'll meet him in the garden. But not a word to anyone else.

SUZANNA: Not even Figaro?

COUNTESS: Particularly him. I don't want his interference. Fetch my velvet facemask and my walking stick. I'll go and think this through on the terrace.

(*SUZANNA goes into the dressing room.*)

I like this plot! Oh! My ribbon! My pretty ribbon. I'd almost forgotten all about you. I shall always keep you as a memory of the moment when the poor pageboy... Oh my Lord! What have you done! And what on earth am I doing?

SUZANNA: (*Re-entering.*) Here's the mask and cane.

COUNTESS: Remember, you're forbidden to tell Figaro.

SUZANNA: Your plan's excellent! It pulls all the threads together, sews them up tightly and brings everything to a proper end. And this time I will get married!

(*SUZANNA kisses the COUNTESS' hand and they exit.*)

End of Act Two.

ACT THREE

The so-called throne-room of the chateau which serves as an audience chamber. On one side there is a dais surmounted by a throne. Above it there is a picture of the King. The COUNT and PEDRILLO, who is dressed in a riding habit and holding a sealed package, are discovered.

COUNT: Did you hear what I said.

PEDRILLO: Yes, my Lord. (*He exits.*)

COUNT: Pedrillo!

PEDRILLO: (*Returning.*) My Lord!

COUNT: Nobody saw you, did they?

PEDRILLO: Not a soul.

COUNT: Take the black stallion.

PEDRILLO: Saddled and waiting at the garden gate.

COUNT: Excellent! Ride hard for Seville.

PEDRILLO: It's only seven miles and the road is good.

COUNT: If the pageboy's already there…

PEDRILLO: …at the barracks?

COUNT: Yes. Find out exactly when he arrived.

PEDRILLO: I understand.

COUNT: Give him his commission and come straight back.

PEDRILLO: What if he's not there?

COUNT: Then come back quicker and let me know.

(*PEDRILLO exits.*

The COUNT wanders up and down thinking.)

Silly of me to send Bazile away like that! Never lose your temper. It doesn't help. What's going on? That letter about the Countess. Is someone after her? The chambermaid locked in and her mistress terrified. Was that genuine or not? One man leaps out of the window and another one comes along swearing he was the one who jumped. But

who knows? No, I'm missing something. I can do what I like with the peasant girls
on my estate. But if one of their men is after the Countess…! What am I saying? I'm letting my imagination run riot. She wouldn't do anything beneath her station. Unlike me. Where has my honour gone? And where do I stand with Suzanna? She hasn't got Figaro yet. Nor he, her. Has she given me away? Oh! How did I ever get caught up in this nightmare? God knows I've wanted to get out of it often enough. If only
I could be more decisive! If I was sure I wanted her
I wouldn't lust after her nearly as much. Come on Figaro. Where are you?

(*FIGARO appears in the distance and stops.*)

I must try to find out subtly whether he knows about my love for Suzie…

FIGARO: (*Aside.*) There he is!

COUNT: …and whether she's breathed a word to him…

FIGARO: (*Aside.*) He suspects me!

COUNT: …that I'm going to marry him off to the old woman.

FIGARO: (*Aside.*) Bazile's loved one!

COUNT: …and keep the young one for myself.

FIGARO: (*Aside.*) He's after my wife, if you please!

COUNT: (*Turning round.*) What! Ah! What are you doing here?

FIGARO: I came at your command, my Lord!

COUNT: What did you mean just now?

FIGARO: My Lord?

COUNT: When you said 'My wife, if you please.'

FIGARO: It was the end of a sentence. 'Go and tell my wife, if you please.'

COUNT: (*Aside.*) 'His wife!' (*Loud.*) Why have you kept me waiting so long?

FIGARO: My clothes got dirty when I jumped into the flowerbeds. I've had to change.

COUNT: In this household the servants take longer to dress than their masters!

FIGARO: That's because they don't have valets to help them.

COUNT: (*Aside.*) Stay calm, Almaviva, or you'll never find out the truth.

FIGARO: (*Aside.*) Careful, Figaro!

COUNT: (*Calmer.*) As you know, I have been thinking of taking you to London as my courier. However, on reflection...

FIGARO: You've changed your mind, my Lord?

COUNT: Well to begin with, you don't know the language.

FIGARO: I know *God damn it.*

COUNT: Pardon?

FIGARO: I said I know *God damn it!*

COUNT: So what?

FIGARO: English is a fine language. You can get so far with so little. Just use *God damn it* and you'll get whatever you want. Fancy a nice fat chicken, for example, go into any tavern, make this gesture to the serving boy. (*He mimes turning a spit.*) Say *God damn it!* and they bring you a joint of salt beef without bread. Quite remarkable. If you want a glass of burgundy or claret there's nothing easier. Just do this! (*He mimes uncorking a bottle.*) Say *God damn it!* and they bring you a foaming flagon of beer. Wonderful! And if you come across a pretty young Lady, mincing along the street with downcast eyes, elbows back, hips gently swinging, grip her firmly by the chin, say *God damn it!* and she'll punch you like a prize-fighter, which just goes to prove that she understands your intentions perfectly. Actually the English do add a sprinkling of one or two other words in the conversation from time to time. But it's quite clear that *God damn it!*

is the basis of their language. So if that's the only reason your Lordship thinks he should leave me in Spain…

COUNT: (*Aside.*) He still wants to come to London. She obviously hasn't told him.

FIGARO: (*Aside.*) He thinks I don't know. I'll play him at his own game.

COUNT: Why would the Countess want to play such a trick on me?

FIGARO: Surely you know her better than me, my Lord.

COUNT: I cater to her every need. She's forever getting gifts from me.

FIGARO: Except the gift of fidelity, my Lord. Do we ever thank those who bestow us with luxuries if they fail to provide us with the necessities?

COUNT: You used to tell me everything.

FIGARO: I have nothing to hide, my Lord.

COUNT: How much did the Countess give you to help her in this little escapade?

FIGARO: How much did you give me to get her out of the Doctor's clutches? Don't abuse a good servant, my Lord, or you risk turning him into a bad one.

COUNT: Then stop behaving so suspiciously.

FIGARO: You smell deception everywhere.

COUNT: And your reputation stinks!

FIGARO: What do you expect? It's a rat race out there. Everybody pushing and shoving, elbowing and trampling. It's every man for himself. Well I've had enough. I'm done with it!

COUNT: Done with ambition? A man with your personality and energy.

FIGARO: Personality and energy? Sycophancy and mediocrity are what get you on in life.

COUNT: I'll teach you the art of politics.

FIGARO: I already know it.

COUNT: As well as you know English!

FIGARO: Understanding politics is nothing to be proud of. Pretending you don't know what you do know; paying attention to things you don't understand and being deaf to things you do; laying claim to power you don't possess. Hiding secrets that don't exist: appearing profound when your mind's vacant; encouraging spies, rewarding traitors; steaming open letters; trying to
boost the lowliness of your status by exaggerating the importance of your purpose. That's politics.

COUNT: What you're talking about is intrigue.

FIGARO: Call it what you like. It's all the same in my book and for those who like the game, let them play. For my own part I prefer to stay 'with me and my girl' as the old song goes.

COUNT: (*Aside.*) He wants to stay here! Suzie must have given me away.

FIGARO: (*Aside.*) That's fooled him.

COUNT: Do you expect to win your case against Marceline?

FIGARO: How could your Lordship condemn me for refusing an old maid when you've pinched all the young ones yourself?

COUNT: In court the judge follows statute. He has to set his own interests to one side.

FIGARO: Lenient on the mighty, strict on the weak.

COUNT: It's no laughing matter.

FIGARO: Of course not, my Lord! But 'truth will out' as they say. We'll see who means me harm and who good.

COUNT: (*Aside.*) He knows everything. He'll have to marry the old spinster.

FIGARO: (*Aside.*) He hasn't found anything out!

SERVANT: (*Entering.*) His Honour, Don Guisman Gosling!

COUNT: Gosling?

FIGARO: Your colleague the local magistrate.

COUNT: Tell him to wait.

> (*The SERVANT exits.*)

FIGARO: (*Watching the COUNT who is lost in thought.*) Does your Excellency need anything?

COUNT: I asked for this room to be laid out for the public hearing.

FIGARO: It's all here. The throne for your Lordship, the comfortable chairs for the magistrates, the stool for the clerk, two benches for the lawyers and the barrier to keep the gentlefolk from the *hoi polloi*. I'll send the cleaners away. (*Exits.*)

COUNT: It's embarrassing he always out-argues me! They're a pair of good-for-nothings. I don't mind them being friends; they can even be lovers but I'm damned if they're going to be husband and wife…

SUZANNA: (*Enters breathlessly.*) I'm sorry to interrupt, my Lord!

COUNT: What's the matter?

SUZANNA: I came to ask you if I could borrow your smelling salts for her Ladyship. She's got the vapours.
As soon as she's finished with them I'll bring them straight back to you.

COUNT: (*Giving them to her.*) You can keep them. You might need them soon.

SUZANNA: Women of my class don't get the vapours. It's a genteel illness confined to the boudoir.

COUNT: (*Musing.*) A fiancée in love, her future in jeopardy…

SUZANNA: Not if we pay Marceline with the dowry you promised me…

COUNT: Promised you?

SUZANNA: That's what you said.

COUNT: Yes, if you would only listen to me.

SUZANNA: It's my duty to listen to everything you say, my Lord, and I do.

COUNT: You're a cruel girl Suzie. Why didn't you say so before?

SUZANNA: Is it too late to say what you want to?

COUNT: Come to the garden at dusk?

SUZANNA: I go there every evening, anyway.

COUNT: Why were you so harsh to me this morning?

SUZANNA: The pageboy was hiding behind the armchair!

COUNT: Of course, I'd forgotten. But why have you refused me so obstinately? Bazile has tried so hard on my behalf.

SUZANNA: Why bother with him?

COUNT: You're right! But what about Figaro? Don't you tell him everything?

SUZANNA: Everything! Except the things I keep to myself!

COUNT: (*Laughing.*) You're enchanting! But let's be clear. Do you promise to come? If you don't keep your word, and there's no rendezvous, then there's no dowry. No dowry, no wedding.

SUZANNA: No wedding, no marriage! No marriage, no *droit de seigneur!*

COUNT: Clever! Where do you get it from? (*Aside.*) She's delicious! (*Loud.*) Isn't your mistress waiting for those salts?

SUZANNA: (*Laughing and giving him back the bottle.*) Of course not. It was just an excuse to talk to you.

COUNT: (*Trying to kiss her.*) Gorgeous creature!

SUZANNA: Somebody's coming.

COUNT: (*Aside.*) She's mine. (*Exits.*)

SUZANNA: I'd better get back to her Ladyship.

FIGARO: (*Entering.*) Suzie! Where are you off to in such a hurry? Wasn't that his Lordship?

SUZANNA: Plead your case and you'll win. (*She runs off.*)

FIGARO: (*Exits following her.*) Just a minute! What do you mean?

COUNT: (*Re-entering.*) 'Plead your case and you'll win.' So it was a trap! Insolence! I'll have you punished in the manner you deserve. Strictly by the law. But suppose he were to pay the old maid...with what...but if he did...? Got it! Antonio's so proud that he hates the idea of his niece marrying Figaro, a servant. I'll encourage that feeling. Why shouldn't I? In the vast field of human intrigue everything should be cultivated. Even an old drunkard's snobbery. (*Calling.*) Antonio. (*Exits.*)

Enter BARTHOLO, MARCELINE and GOSLING.

MARCELINE: (*To GOSLING.*) Hear my case, monsieur.

GOSLING: (*Stammering.*) Very w-w-well. Let's hear what you have to say. Verbally!

BARTHOLO: It's about a breach of a promise.

MARCELINE: And a loan default.

GOSLING: I quite understand. With the usual consequences.

MARCELINE: No. The consequences are most unusual.

GOSLING: I quite understand. You don't want to repay the money.

MARCELINE: No. It was me who lent it.

GOSLING: I quite understand. And now you want it b-b-back?

MARCELINE: No. I want him to marry me.

GOSLING: I quite understand. Does he want to marry you?

MARCELINE: No Señor. That's what the case is about.

GOSLING: Do you think I don't understand the case?

MARCELINE: No sir! (*To BARTHOLO.*) Help. (*To GOSLING.*) Are you really a judge?

GOSLING: I should be. I p-p-paid enough to become one.

MARCELINE: The sale of offices is an abuse of the system.

GOSLING: I couldn't agree with you more. I think we should get them for nothing. Now whom are you accusing?

(*Enter FIGARO, rubbing his hands.*)

MARCELINE: This wretched man.

FIGARO: Have I upset you? His Lordship will be here in a moment, Your Honour.

GOSLING: Have I seen you somewhere before, young man?

FIGARO: At your wife's house, Your Honour. I was in her service.

GOSLING: When was that?

FIGARO: Just under a year before the birth of your youngest son. A very handsome child he is too, if I may say so.

GOSLING: He's the b-b-best looking of the lot. I understand you've been getting up to your old tricks again.

FIGARO: Oh no, this is just minor.

GOSLING: Promises of marriage are never minor.

FIGARO: Señor…

GOSLING: Have you seen my secretary, young man?

FIGARO: Do you mean Underhand, the clerk of the Court?

GOSLING: That's it. He does both jobs.

FIGARO: And he has a hand in the tills! Yes, I've given him the depositions and the supplementary statements. All the standard stuff.

GOSLING: In the judicial process, the forms are paramount.

FIGARO: Of course, señor. How else would the lawyers make their money.

GOSLING: You're not as green as I thought. Well since you know so much about the law we'd better take a particular interest in your case.

FIGARO: I rely on your integrity, Your Honour, even though you are a judge.

GOSLING: What? Yes, I am a judge. Now, I understand you owe a sum of money and won't pay it?

FIGARO: I think the Counsellor will soon be of the opinion that I never owed a peseta.

GOSLING: Quite so. What? What did he say?

(*Enter an USHER followed by the COUNT.*)

USHER: Gentlemen, his Excellency!

COUNT: In full regalia Gosling! This is only a local case, a domestic matter. You needn't have bothered.

GOSLING: You're too gracious, my Lord, but I wear my r-r-robes everywhere I go. They may sn-snigger at a magistrate in a short t-t-tunic but they tremble at the sight of a judge in robes.

COUNT: (*To the USHER.*) Let the public in.

USHER: (*Opening the door.*) Enter the court!

(*UNDERHAND, ANTONIO, various SERVANTS and PEASANTS enter and take their places at the rear of the Court. The COUNT sits on the throne, GOSLING next to him. UNDERHAND is on a stool behind the table. The MAGISTRATES and LAWYERS are on benches. MARCELINE is next to BARTHOLO. FIGARO sits opposite them on the other bench.*)

GOSLING: (*To UNDERHAND.*) Underhand, read out the details of the case.

UNDERHAND: Barbe-Agar-Raab-Madeleine-Nicole-Marceline de Vino-Verde, spinster; versus Figaro…no Christian name supplied.

FIGARO: Anonymous.

GOSLING: Anonymous! Not a p-p-patron saint I know.

FIGARO: My very own.

UNDERHAND: (*Pen in hand.*) Versus Anonymous Figaro. Rank or title?

FIGARO: Gentleman.

COUNT: You're a gentleman?

FIGARO: The son of a prince had heaven so intended.

COUNT: Get on with it.

USHER: Silence in court!

UNDERHAND: In the matter of the marriage of the aforesaid Figaro brought by the aforesaid Vino-Verde, Dr Bartholo represents the plaintiff and if the Court allows, even though it be contrary to the practice, habit and custom of the Court, the aforesaid Anonymous Figaro will represent himself.

FIGARO: Practice, habits and customs can often be abused, Señor Underhand. Even a mildly intelligent plaintiff understands his own case better than an advocate who has to start everything from scratch. The lawyer knows everything except the details of his client's brief. So he pleads at the top of his voice and doesn't mind ruining his case, boring the court and sending the magistrates off to sleep. I, on the other hand, can put my case in a few simple words.

UNDERHAND: But you aren't the plaintiff. You're here to defend yourself. Doctor, come forward and read out the promissory note of marriage.

FIGARO: Yes the promise!

BARTHOLO: It's unambiguous.

GOSLING: Then read it out.

UNDERHAND: Silence, gentlemen!

USHER: Silence in court!

BARTHOLO: 'I the undersigned having received from Senorita Marceline de Vino-Verde in the chateau of Aguas-Frescas the sum of two thousand Spanish piasters agree to return the same to her on demand and in consideration of which I will marry her in the castle
etc.' It's signed simply, Figaro. We, the plaintiff, claim restitution of the money and execution of the undertaking,

with costs. Gentlemen, never since Alexander the Great promised to marry the beautiful Thalestris was there a more interesting case submitted to the arbitration of the courts…

COUNT: (*Interrupting.*) Before you go any further Doctor, is there any doubt about the validity of the document?

GOSLING: (*To FIGARO.*) Do you have anything to say about that?

FIGARO: Gentlemen, there was malice, mistake and misrepresentation in the way in which the undertaking was read out. It doesn't say 'and in consideration of which' but 'or in consideration of which I will marry her.' There is a difference.

COUNT: Does it say 'and' or 'or' in the document?

BARTHOLO: It says 'and'.

FIGARO: 'Or.'

GOSLING: Underhand, you read it.

UNDERHAND: (*Taking the document.*) Yes indeed. Interested parties often misrepresent words when they read things aloud. 'Senorita de Vino-Verde…agree to return the same to her on demand and…or…and, or.' The word's badly written…and there's a blot.

BARTHOLO: I maintain that the word used is the copulative conjunction 'and' which links the two member sub-clauses in the body of the sentence. 'I will return the money' and 'I will marry her.'

FIGARO: I, on the other hand, maintain that it's the abortive conjunctus interruptus 'or' which separates the so-called members from joining into one body. What's more, if this pedant wants to start spouting Latin, I'll talk Greek and walk all over him.

COUNT: How are we to make a judgement in such a matter?

BARTHOLO: We don't want to quibble about a little word and are prepared to concede that if there is a word there it is 'or'.

FIGARO: Write that down, Underhand.

BARTHOLO: Certainly but that won't save you. Let's examine the document without the word at all. 'I agree to return the same to her on demand in consideration of which I will marry her in the castle' In other words 'my reward to you for the loan of the money is marriage'. What could be clearer? The blot is a blot. That's all there is to it. There is no word underneath. It hides nothing.

FIGARO: On the contrary. The blot hides a plot. Do you think it likely gentlemen that I would allow my quill to blot such an important word? No. It was deliberately blotted by someone else. Besides if there were no word underneath then there would be a comma after the word consideration. Is there such a comma?

BARTHOLO: There is no comma.

FIGARO: Then the word 'or' *was* underneath.

(*The JUDGES rise and talk amongst themselves.*)

BARTHOLO: (*To FIGARO.*) A fine defence!

UNDERHAND: Silence, gentlemen.

USHER: Silence in court!

BARTHOLO: (*To FIGARO.*) A very gentlemanly way of settling your debts!

FIGARO: Are you pleading your own cause?

BARTHOLO: Of course not! I'm speaking on behalf of this Lady.

FIGARO: Then cut out the insults! When the law allowed third parties to appear on behalf of litigants, they were not expected to be abusive. It's contempt of court.

(*The JUDGES continue to talk amongst themselves.*)

ANTONIO: (*To MARCELINE, pointing at the judges.*) What are they babbling about?

MARCELINE: Somebody's got at the judge. Now he's corrupting the Count I think I am going to lose my case.

BARTHOLO: (*Aside.*) I am afraid you're right.

FIGARO: Courage, Marceline!

UNDERHAND: (*To MARCELINE.*) Silence.

COUNT: Here is the court's decision. The plaintiff is entitled to marriage in default of payment; marriage *and* payment are incompatible.

UNDERHAND: Silence, gentlemen.

USHER: Silence in court!

COUNT: As to the defendant. He wishes to remain free and may do so.

FIGARO: I've won.

COUNT: But the document says, he agrees 'to return the money on demand or in consideration of which he will marry her'. The Court therefore orders the defendant to pay the two thousand piasters to the plaintiff or to marry her today.

FIGARO: I've lost.

ANTONIO: Great!

FIGARO: What do you mean great?

ANTONIO: Because you're not going to become my nephew. Many thanks, my Lord.

USHER: Clear the court!

ANTONIO: I must go and tell my niece.

(*The courtroom empties leaving the COUNT, MARCELINE, BARTHOLO, FIGARO and GOSLING.*)

MARCELINE: I can breathe again.

FIGARO: I'm suffocating.

COUNT: (*Aside.*) I've got my own back.

FIGARO: (*Aside.*) Where's Bazile? He was supposed to be here to raise an objection to my marriage with Marceline? (*To the COUNT.*) You're not leaving us are you, my Lord?

COUNT: The judgement is delivered.

FIGARO: I can't marry Marceline. I am a gentleman.

BARTHOLO: You *will* marry her.

FIGARO: Without my noble parents' consent?

BARTHOLO: Bring them here. Let's see them.

FIGARO: Give me a chance. I've only been looking for fifteen years.

BARTHOLO: Idiot! You were probably found on a doorstep.

FIGARO: Not found, doctor. Lost or rather stolen.

COUNT: Where's your proof?

FIGARO: My Lord! The lace shawl, the embroidered clothes and the gold trinkets found on me. They're all quite clear indications that I am of noble birth. Besides somebody took the precaution of tattooing me. Here on my arm! This must mean I was a valued child. (*He rolls up his sleeve.*)

MARCELINE: Not a spatula?

FIGARO: How do you know that?

MARCELINE: My God! It's him!

FIGARO: Of course it's me.

BARTHOLO: Who do you mean, him?

MARCELINE: It's little Emmanuel!

BARTHOLO: (*To FIGARO.*) Were you kidnapped by a band of gypsies?

FIGARO: Very close to a castle. Doctor, if you can re-unite me with my family, you can name your price. My parents would pay you anything.

BARTHOLO: (*Indicating MARCELINE.*) Figaro, this is your mother.

FIGARO: My wet nurse?

BARTHOLO: The real thing.

COUNT: His mother!

FIGARO: Tell me more.

MARCELINE: (*Indicating BARTHOLO.*) And this is your father.

FIGARO: God help me!

MARCELINE: Hasn't nature told you a thousand times?

FIGARO: Not once.

COUNT: (*Aside.*) His mother!

GOSLING: Clearly he can't m-m-marry her now.

BARTHOLO: Nor me!

MARCELINE: Nor you? But your son – you swore…

BARTHOLO: If I got married for every slip I've made I'd be doing it all the time.

GOSLING: And if everyone behaved like you – no-one would ever get married.

BARTHOLO: You had a scandalous youth.

MARCELINE: Yes, it's true my youth was scandalous. But for twenty years since, I've lived virtuously in repentance. And why should I be the only one to repent, I was poor, young and innocent; at the mercy of men. They should be condemned for all the women they have ruined.

FIGARO: The guilty ones are always the least generous.

MARCELINE: Generous! You despise the women you lusted after. Even in society we're treated like objects. You pretend to respect and love us but you handle us like slaves or children, then you punish us like adults. Don't you see why you disgust us?

FIGARO: She's right!

COUNT: (*Aside.*) She's too right!

GOSLING: She's absolutely right!

MARCELINE: So never mind this unjust man. The past is over. Look to the future. Now you will have a loving wife and a loving mother. The only disagreement will be over who loves you most. Be happy, my son, be kind to us, and good and generous to the world. That's all your mother asks.

FIGARO: Mother, everything you say is pure gold.

COUNT: (*Aside.*) This is going to upset my plans.

GOSLING: What about the noble birth? The castle? Trying to hoodwink justice were you?

FIGARO: And look how she's rewarded me. How many times have I nearly strangled this man because I owed him a hundred pesetas. And today I discover he's my father! But I'm sorry Daddy. Mummy, please kiss me. As maternally as you can.

(*MARCELINE embraces him as SUZANNA runs in with a purse in her hand.*)

SUZANNA: My Lord, stop! Don't let them get married! I've come to repay the lady with money her Ladyship has given me.

COUNT: (*Aside.*) Damn my wife! They're all in it together.

ANTONIO: (*Entering and indicating MARCELINE with her arms around FIGARO.*) You're too late young lady!

SUZANNA: Alright! I've seen enough. Let's go, uncle.

FIGARO: Please don't go. What do you think you've seen?

SUZANNA: My stupidity and your betrayal!

FIGARO: Wrong on both counts!

SUZANNA: I hope you have a happy marriage.

FIGARO: We are happy but we're not going to get married.

(*SUZANNA tries to go but FIGARO holds her back.*)

SUZANNA: You dare to try and keep me here!

FIGARO: (*To the others.*) Not very affectionate, is she? (*To SUZANNA.*) Before you go, just take a look at this lady.

SUZANNA: I'm looking.

FIGARO: And what do you see?

SUZANNA: A horror!

FIGARO: Ah jealousy! You can always rely on it.

MARCELINE: Embrace your mother, my sweet Suzanna. The wicked man tormenting you, is my son.

SUZANNA: You're his mother?

(*They embrace.*)

ANTONIO: Is this really happening?

FIGARO: I think so.

MARCELINE: I knew I was drawn to him but I didn't realise it was the call of blood.

FIGARO: And I couldn't have disliked you, mother. I may have refused your offer of marriage but I still borrowed your money.

MARCELINE: (*Giving him the document.*) It's yours now. A wedding present.

SUZANNA: (*Throwing him the purse.*) And there's this too.

FIGARO: Thank you very much.

MARCELINE: I was an unhappy girl and I nearly became an even more miserable wife. Instead of which, I am the most fortunate of mothers. Kiss me children. Let me rejoice in your affection. Is it possible to be this happy? Oh you'll see how I shall love you both!

FIGARO: (*Moved.*) Steady on mother! I've never cried before. At least they're tears of joy. Silly of me! I was almost ashamed of them. I felt them trickling through my fingers and tried to hide them! I want to laugh and cry at the same time. I'll never feel like this again.

MARCELINE: My dear!

SUZANNA: And mine!

(*They kiss MARCELINE on both cheeks.*)

GOSLING: (*Drying his eyes.*) I think I'm going soft too!

FIGARO: (*Carried away.*) I defy you sadness! With these two women as my guardian angels.

ANTONIO: (*To FIGARO.*) Oh please! You can't marry into my family unless your parents are married first. Have yours tied the knot?

BARTHOLO: I'm not knotting anything with her. She's his mother!

ANTONIO: So you're an illegitimate father! (*To FIGARO.*) Forget it.

SUZANNA: Uncle...

ANTONIO: I am not giving my sister's daughter away to a young man who has no father.

GOSLING: Don't be stupid everyone's got a father!

ANTONIO: He shan't have her – ever! (*Exits.*)

BARTHOLO: (*To FIGARO.*) You'd better look for someone to adopt you. (*He tries to leave.*)

MARCELINE: (*Runs after BARTHOLO and takes his arm.*) Please, Doctor, don't go.

FIGARO: (*Aside.*) All the idiots in Andalucia are trying to stop my marriage.

SUZANNA: (*To BARTHOLO.*) This is your son.

MARCELINE: (*To BARTHOLO.*) In mind, in spirit, and in looks!

FIGARO: (*To BARTHOLO.*) And he hasn't cost you a peseta!

BARTHOLO: What about the hundred crowns he stole from me?

MARCELINE: (*Stroking him.*) We'll take such care of you, papa!

SUZANNA: (*Stroking him.*) We'll show you such love and tenderness, daddy!

BARTHOLO: (*Moved.*) Father! Papa! Daddy! (*Indicating GOSLING.*) I'm becoming as daft as that dotard. I'm behaving like a child.

(*MARCELINE and SUZANNA kiss him.*)

No! I haven't said yes yet. What's happened to his Lordship?

FIGARO: Let's get to him quickly. He can give us his blessing! We don't want him to start plotting again or we'll be back where we started.

ALL: Quick. Let's go. (*Etc.*)

(*They drag BARTHOLO with them and all exit except GOSLING.*)

GOSLING: 'D-D-Daft as that d-d-dotard' indeed! How uncouth…they really are very impolite round here! (*Exits.*)

End of Act Three.

ACT FOUR

A saloon lit by candelabras and festooned with garlands and bouquets. It has been made ready for a party. There is a writing desk with an armchair behind it downstage left. FIGARO and SUZANNA are discovered.

FIGARO: Are you happy now darling? The Doctor's won over by my silver-tongued mother. He's going to marry her and your uncle's silenced. Isn't it wonderful?

SUZANNA: It's strange though.

FIGARO: No, it's wonderful! We only wanted one dowry, now we've got two – no thanks to his lordship. You had a rival who was driving me mad, what happens? She turns into my loving mother. Yesterday I was an orphan, today I've got two parents. Not quite as rich as I imagined, but then too much money corrupts.

SUZANNA: But none of it is what you actually planned!

FIGARO: Fate did better than us. That's how it goes. You plan, you scheme one way, fate decides another way. As for the God of love…

SUZANNA: He's the one I'm interested in.

FIGARO: I'll bring him to our house and make him our lodger for ever.

SUZANNA: And won't you ever look for any other home?

FIGARO: If you ever found I'd strayed you could take a thousand million lovers…

SUZANNA: Stop exaggerating! Tell the truth.

FIGARO: It is the truth, my darling!

SUZANNA: Then there must be more than one kind.

FIGARO: Oh there are hundreds of varieties! Some you know but daren't give breath to because some truths should never be said. Others you uphold but don't believe in. Some are completely unacceptable… Lovers' vows, mothers' threats, drunkards' resolutions, political promises, a businessman's word – there's no end to them. The only one you can have faith in is my love for Suzie.

SUZANNA: All I know is I'm only going to love my husband.

FIGARO: Keep your word and you'll be the exception to the rule.

SUZANNA: Now about my little tryst with the Count.

FIGARO: Forget it. Let him freeze his aristocratic derrière.

SUZANNE: Agreed.

(*He tries to kiss her. The COUNTESS enters intercepting the kiss.*)

COUNTESS: I was right. I said I'd find you together. Come on Figaro, what about the wedding? Everybody's waiting. They're getting impatient.

FIGARO: I was forgetting myself, my Lady. I'll go and tender my apologies. (*He tries to drag SUZANNA with him.*)

COUNTESS: (*Holding her.*) She'll follow you later.

(*FIGARO exits.*)

Have you arranged our disguises?

SUZANNA: There's no need my Lady. The rendezvous is off.

COUNTESS: You haven't changed your mind?

SUZANNA: No, but Figaro has.

COUNTESS: You're lying.

SUZANNA: I swear I'm not.

COUNTESS: Are you really trying to tell me that Figaro would let a dowry like this slip through his fingers.

SUZANNA: What do you mean, my Lady?

COUNTESS: I see what's happened! You've made it up with the Count and you're sorry you told me what he's up to. I see through you, Suzanna. Well go on. Leave me alone!

(*The COUNTESS tries to leave, but SUZANNA blocks her way, throwing herself on her knees in front of her.*)

SUZANNA: In Heaven's name, my Lady, you do me wrong! Do you really think I'd do such a thing after all you've done for me, the dowry you've given me…

COUNTESS: (*Raising her.*) I'm sorry. I don't know what came over me. Why don't you let me take your place in the garden? That way you'll keep faith with your husband and help me get mine back.

SUZANNA: You've really upset me!

COUNTESS: I was stupid. I'm sorry. (*She kisses her on the forehead.*) Where is the rendezvous?

SUZANNA: He said the garden.

COUNTESS: Paper and pen, quick! Let's fix a place.

SUZANNA: Do you mean, write to him?

COUNTESS: What else?

SUZANNA: (*Sits at the writing desk.*) But shouldn't it be in your Ladyship's writing?

COUNTESS: (*As the COUNTESS begins to dictate.*) There's a new song I've heard. It goes:

'When it's dark at night, and the stars are shining
Under the horse-chestnuts I'll be pining…'

SUZANNA: (*Writing.*) Under the horse-chestnuts…is that all?

COUNTESS: Don't you think it's specific enough?

SUZANNA: (*Reading it again.*) It's fine. (*Folding the note.*) What shall we seal it with?

COUNTESS: Pin it. Quick, use this. He can attach it to the reply. Write on the back: 'return the pin'.

SUZANNA: (*Laughing.*) This is even better than the business with the commission. Do you remember, my Lady?

COUNTESS: (*Sadly.*) Oh yes!

SUZANNA: I haven't got a pin.

COUNTESS: Take this one. (*In undoing her dress the ribbon falls out.*) Oops!

SUZANNA: (*Picking it up.*) Isn't that the ribbon the page stole? You don't mean to keep it from him?

COUNTESS: It wouldn't have been right to have left it tied on his arm, would it? Let me have it back.

SUZANNA: Stained with the young man's blood?

COUNTESS: (*Snatching it.*) Fanchette will adore it. I'll give it her the next time she brings me flowers.

(*CHERUBINO enters dressed as a shepherdess. FANCHETTE and some other girls carrying bouquets accompany him.*)

FANCHETTE: My Lady, the village girls have come to present you with flowers.

COUNTESS: (*Putting away the ribbon.*) How charming! I'm so sorry that I don't know who you all are. (*Indicating CHERUBINO.*) Who is this fair child? Such a modest countenance?

SHEPHERDESS: She's a cousin of mine, my Lady. She's just come for the wedding.

COUNTESS: She's very pretty. I can only hold one bouquet so let's honour our visitor. (*She takes CHERUBINO's bouquet and kisses his forehead.*) She's blushing, Suzanna. Doesn't she remind you of someone?

SUZANNA: The resemblance is uncanny.

CHERUBINO: (*Aside, hands on heart.*) How I've longed for that kiss.

(*Enter ANTONIO and the COUNT.*)

ANTONIO: I tell you he's here, my Lord. He used my daughter's room to dress in. His uniform's still there and here's his soldier's cap that I picked up off the floor. (*He looks along the line of girls, recognises CHERUBINO and takes off his bonnet so that his long hair falls to his shoulders. He replaces the bonnet with the soldier's cap.*) Well, well! If it isn't our officer!

COUNTESS: Good heavens!

SUZANNA: The rascal!

ANTONIO: I told you he was here somewhere.

COUNT: What is the meaning of this, my Lady?

COUNTESS: I am as surprised as you are, and every bit as vexed.

COUNT: And this morning?

COUNTESS: I won't pretend any longer. It's true that he came to my room and together we planned the joke that these youngsters have played. While we were dressing him up, you interrupted us and you were so enraged that he escaped through the window. I was upset and shock did the rest.

COUNT: (*To CHERUBINO.*) Why didn't you leave the chateau when I told you to?

CHERUBINO: (*Doffing his cap.*) My Lord...

COUNT: Your disobedience shan't go unpunished.

FANCHETTE: Please, my Lord, may I speak? You know the way when you're trying to kiss me you always say, 'You can have anything you want from me my dear little Fanchette, if only you'll love me.'?

COUNT: I don't know what you mean.

FANCHETTE: Surely you do, my Lord! Don't punish Cherubino, give him to me in marriage and I promise I'll love you till the cows come home.

COUNT: (*Aside.*) That boy has done it again!

COUNTESS: (*Repeating his question.*) Well, señor. You have no reason to be suspicious about my behaviour but after her testimony I have every reason to be suspicious of yours.

ANTONIO: You too, my Lord. I don't know! Like her late mother God rest her soul. It doesn't matter. I'll have to teach her what's right while she's young but as my Lady knows when little girls grow up...!

COUNT: (*Aside.*) There's some evil genius against me!

FIGARO: (*Enters.*) My Lord, if you're going to keep the young ladies any longer, there'll be no wedding breakfast and no dancing.

COUNT: Dancing! I thought you sprained your ankle this morning.

FIGARO: (*Rubbing his leg.*) I'm still suffering my Lord, but I'm over the worst. (*To the girls.*) Come on girls.

COUNT: You were lucky that the flowerbeds were so soft, weren't you?

FIGARO: Very.

ANTONIO: And he curled himself up into a ball when he jumped.

FIGARO: With a bit more practice I'd have stayed up in the air! (*To the girls.*) Off we go ladies.

ANTONIO: And while you were jumping, the little page was galloping off to Seville.

FIGARO: Galloping or maybe trotting!

COUNT: And you had his commission in your pocket?

FIGARO: (*A little surprised.*) Of course. Why so many questions? Come along, girls!

ANTONIO: (*Pulling CHERUBINO by the arm.*) There's somebody here who says my future nephew's a liar.

FIGARO: Cherubino! (*Aside.*) What's he doing here?

ANTONIO: Now what do you say?

FIGARO: What do I say…I say…what's his story?

COUNT: He says *he* jumped into the melon bed.

FIGARO: Well if he says so, he says so.

COUNT: Then you and him?

FIGARO: When your Excellency's angry most people would prefer to risk a broken limb or two.

COUNT: You mean both of you jumped?

FIGARO: It's all the rage nowadays.

COUNT: What, two at the same time?

FIGARO: If there were two dozen, we'd have done it. And what's the harm? No-one was hurt. (*To the girls.*) Now ladies, let's go!

COUNT: (*Outraged.*) Does he think this is a comedy?

(*A fanfare off.*)

FIGARO: That's the signal for the procession. To your positions ladies. Suzie, take my arm please.

(*All exit leaving CHERUBINO, the COUNT and COUNTESS behind.*)

COUNT: (*Looking after FIGARO.*) The audacity of the man! As for you, pretending to be ashamed of yourself, go and get changed and don't let me catch sight of you for the rest of the evening.

COUNTESS: He'll be so bored.

CHERUBINO: With what's on my forehead I could be happy for the rest of my life. (*He exits.*)

COUNT: What has he got on his forehead?

COUNTESS: His soldier's cap. War's a game to a boy of his age. (*She makes to leave.*)

COUNT: You're not going, are you?

COUNTESS: You know I'm not well.

COUNT: Stay, at least for Suzanna's sake, or I'll think you're angry with me.

COUNTESS: Here come the wedding parties!

COUNT: (*Aside.*) I can't stop it so I'll have to put up with it.

(*The bridal parties enter to the march from Les Folies d'Espagne. The order of the procession is as follows:*

HUNTSMEN with rifles on their shoulders.

The ALGUAZIL, the MAGISTRATURE and GOSLING.

The PEASANTS in holiday costume.

Two young GIRLS carrying SUZANNA's bridal crown made from white feathers.

Two other young GIRLS carrying the bridal veil.

ANTONIO leading SUZANNA by the hand as the man who is to give the bride away.

Four more young GIRLS carrying MARCELINE's crown and veil.

FIGARO leading MARCELINE by the hand as the man who is to give the bride away to BARTHOLO who is the last to enter and carries a large bouquet.

As the young GIRLS pass the COUNT, they hand to his valets the veils and crowns intended for SUZANNA and MARCELINE.

The village MEN and WOMEN, having taken up positions on opposite sides of the stage, dance a fandango accompanied by castanets. During this dance ANTONIO leads SUZANNA to the COUNT. She kneels in front of him. While the COUNT dresses her in her veil and crown and gives her a bouquet two young GIRLS sing the following.)

GIRLS: Young bride to be sing the glory and praise
Of your Lord who's renounced and forsaken old ways.
He guides you to bed as only he can
As a pure virgin, chaste for your man.

(SUZANNA still on her knees, pulls the COUNT's cloak and shows him the letter she's holding. She secretes it under her veil and the COUNT in adjusting the veil takes the letter. He puts it inside his waistcoat. The song concludes and SUZANNA rises curtseying deeply to the COUNT. FIGARO receives her from the COUNT's hands and they go to the other side of the room near MARCELINE. The COUNT comes downstage to read the letter but in drawing it out of his waistcoat he pricks his finger. He shakes it, presses and sucks it.)

COUNT: Why do women stick pins in everything!

FIGARO: (*To MARCELINE and SUZANNA.*) It's a love letter from some girl. Look, he's pricked himself on the pin that fastened it.

COUNT: (*Reading.*) 'Return the pin.'

The dance is resumed. He looks for the pin on the ground, picks it up and sticks it in his sleeve.

FIGARO: (*To MARCELINE and SUZANNA.*) Anything from a lover is precious! Look at him searching for the pin! Extraordinary!

(*SUZANNA exchanges signals with the COUNTESS. The dance finishes and the choral singing resumes. FIGARO leads MARCELINE to the COUNT and a repetition of the ceremony commences.*

BAZILE enters, guitar in hand, with SUNBURN.)

BAZILE: Lovers true despise all those
Whose love is fickle and fey.
But what care I when I espy
A maid who seems to stay.
And play with me and stay with me
And play with me and stay!
If Cupid's arrows have got a tip
It's so they can go prick, prick, prick
If Cupid's arrows have got a tip
It's so they can go prick...

FIGARO: Don Bazile, why are you singing in the streets?

BAZILE: (*Pointing to SUNBURN.*) To entertain this gentleman as his Lordship ordered.

SUNBURN: With those old songs! Don't make me laugh!

BAZILE: I have shown my loyalty now I ask for justice.

COUNT: What do you want, Bazile?

BAZILE: The hand of Marceline in marriage, my Lord. I've also come to voice my opposition to this...

FIGARO: (*Looking BAZILE in the face.*) Look into my eyes and you'll see a fool.

BAZILE: Exactly.

FIGARO: It's your own reflection. Señor take heed of my warning. If you come anywhere near my Lady...

BARTHOLO: (*Laughing.*) Stop Figaro. Let's hear what he has to say.

GOSLING: Can't you two be friends...?

FIGARO: Us!

BAZILE: Never!

FIGARO: He writes such boring ballads!

BAZILE: His verses don't rhyme.

FIGARO: Tavern singer!

BAZILE: Second stringer!

FIGARO: Wobbling warbler!

BAZILE: Diplomatic bag!

COUNT: Aren't they rude.

BAZILE: He never shows me any respect.

FIGARO: You don't deserve any.

BAZILE: He blackens my reputation at any excuse…

FIGARO: I don't need an excuse.

BAZILE: You see what I mean!

FIGARO: If you can't bear the truth why come to upset our wedding?

BAZILE: (*To MARCELINE.*) Answer me yes or no, didn't you promise me that if you hadn't married within four years you would give me first refusal?

MARCELINE: Not unconditionally.

BAZILE: I did agree to adopt the son that you lost if you found him.

ALL: She's found him.

BAZILE: Impossible.

ALL: It's Figaro.

BAZILE: The devil!

GOSLING: I assume you'll renounce your claim on his mother.

BAZILE: What could be worse than being thought of as the father of a scoundrel?

FIGARO: Being his son.

BAZILE: As this gentleman has become a somebody, I must be a nobody. (*Exits.*)

BARTHOLO: (*Laughing.*) Ha, ha, ha!

FIGARO: (*Jumping with joy.*) At last I am going to get my wife.

COUNT: (*Aside.*) And I, my mistress.

GOSLING: (*Aside.*) Now everybody's happy!

COUNT: Prepare both contracts so that I may sign them.

ALL: Hurrah! (*Exeunt.*)

COUNT: (*Making to go off.*) I need some time on my own.

SUNBURN: (*To FIGARO.*) I'm going to help prepare the firework display under the horse-chestnut trees.

COUNT: (*Returning.*) Who told you to set them up there.

FIGARO: What's the matter?

COUNT: The Countess is indisposed. Put the display on the terrace where she can watch it from her room.

FIGARO: You heard Sunburn. On the terrace!

(*SUNBURN exits.*)

COUNT: Under the horse chestnut trees indeed! (*Aside as he exits.*) They were going to light up my rendezvous!

FIGARO: He's very concerned about his wife all of a sudden!

MARCELINE: Figaro! I have something on my conscience that I'd like to clear up. It's about Suzanna. Although Bazile always maintained the opposite, I misguidedly believed that she had a…an understanding with the Count.

FIGARO: It's a normal female impulse. Why should it upset me? You don't know your son very well, mother.
I defy the cleverest of women to try and take me in.

MARCELINE: It's always better to think the worst, son. Jealousy…

FIGARO: …is the child of pride; or the idiot's illness. It doesn't worry me mother. I can be quite philosophical about it. If Suzie should deceive me, I forgive her in advance. (*He turns and sees FANCHETTE.*) It's my little cousin and she's eavesdropping.

FANCHETTE: No, I'm not. That's not a nice thing to do. I was looking to see if anybody was here.

FIGARO: Cherubino?

FANCHETTE: I know where he is. It's Suzanna I want.

FIGARO: What for?

FANCHETTE: Since you have become my cousin I'll tell you. I wanted to give her back a pin.

FIGARO: (*Angry.*) A pin! What pin! Who gave it to you, you little slut? I'm sorry. (*He calms down.*) I'm sure you're only doing exactly what you were told. You're just being kind, aren't you?

FANCHETTE: Then why are you getting so angry with me. I'm off.

FIGARO: Only joking! I know that pin very well. It's the one the Count told you to give back to Suzie. It was used to hold together a note he'd been given. There, you see, I know it all.

FANCHETTE: So why ask?

FIGARO: I wanted to know what his Lordship said when he asked you to run the errand.

FANCHETTE: Just like you said: 'Fanchette, take this pin to your lovely cousin and tell her it's the key to the horse-chestnuts.'

FIGARO: 'The horse-'…?

FANCHETTE: 'Chestnuts.' Oh, and he added, 'be careful nobody sees you.'

FIGARO: Fortunately no one has. Obey him to the letter and get on with your errand. Remember to let Suzie know precisely what his Lordship told you to say.

FANCHETTE: What else would I say? I'm not a baby. (*Exits.*)

FIGARO: Oh mother! (*His hand on his chest.*) My heart's on the ground.

MARCELINE: It was up in the air a few minutes ago. Can a little pin have deflated it so easily?

FIGARO: But it's the same pin he picked up off the floor, mother.

MARCELINE: (*Recalling his words.*) 'Jealousy…is the child of pride or the idiot's illness. It doesn't worry me mother. I can be quite philosophical about it.'

FIGARO: So that's why the Count was so anxious about the fireworks! My young bride and her pin have got a surprise coming. She and her horse-chestnuts! I'm obviously deep enough into this marriage to make me feel pain, but not so deep that I can't leave and marry someone else.

MARCELINE: Very philosophical! What proof have you that she's deceiving you and not the Count? You've passed sentence without a trial! You don't even know whether she'll turn up under the horse chestnuts. Or if she does, what she's going to say and do. I thought you had more sense.

FIGARO: (*Kissing her hand.*) You're right, of course! Mothers always are! But I always feel better when I've let off steam. I'll see what she does first and frame my actions accordingly. I know where the rendezvous is. Goodbye mother. (*Exits.*)

MARCELINE: I know the rendezvous too. Now I've dealt with him, I'd better go and warn Suzanna. She's such a lovely girl! When we're not fighting each other over personal interests, we poor oppressed women must stick together against these proud, dreadful men. They're such idiots! (*Exits.*)

End of Act Four.

ACT FIVE

A grove of horse chestnuts whose foliage canopies the stage. There are two pavilions, left and right; upstage there is a an ornamental entrance to the garden and downstage a bench. It is dark.

FANCHETTE enters with two biscuits and an orange in one hand and an illuminated paper lantern in the other.

FANCHETTE: The pavilion on the left, he said. That must be this one. What if my little friend doesn't turn up? Those people in the kitchen! They were so horrid.
They wouldn't even give me these without a cross-examination. 'Who are they for?' 'Just someone I know.' 'Oh yes, we all know who that is!' Well I don't care if they do know. Just because his Lordship can't stand the sight of him doesn't mean to say he has to die of hunger. I hope he likes biscuits! They cost me a great smacking kiss. Oh well he can always pay me back. (*She sees FIGARO entering and screams.*) Ah! (*She runs into the kiosk on the left.*)

FIGARO: Fanchette!

(*FIGARO is wearing a large overcoat and a big hat pulled down over his ears. He is accompanied by BAZILE, ANTONIO, BARTHOLO, GOSLING, SUNBURN and a group of SERVANTS and other WORKERS.*)

Gentlemen! Are we all here?

BAZILE: Everybody you asked to come is.

FIGARO: What time is it roughly?

ANTONIO: (*Looking up.*) The moon should be up by now.

BARTHOLO: You look like a conspirator. What dark deeds are you plotting?

FIGARO: Didn't you all come to the chateau for a wedding?

GOSLING: We d-d-did.

ANTONIO: We were in the park to wait for the signal for the celebration to begin.

FIGARO: You don't need to go that far, gentlemen. Here, under the horse chestnuts we're going to honour my virtuous fiancée and the man who wants her for himself.

BAZILE: (*Recalling the events of the day.*) I know what's going on! I suggest we get out of here, gentlemen. It's where the rendezvous is about to take place. I'll tell you all about it, but somewhere else.

GOSLING: (*To FIGARO.*) We'll come back later.

FIGARO: When you hear me shout, come running and if I don't show you something very special, you can do what you like with me.

BARTHOLO: Be warned! The wise man meddles with the aristocracy at his peril.

FIGARO: I'll remember.

BARTHOLO: Their status always gives them the advantage over us.

FIGARO: And their cunning! But that's no reason to be weak. Otherwise you're at the mercy of every villain.

BARTHOLO: That's true.

FIGARO: And that on my mother's side I bear the honoured name of Vino-Verde.

BARTHOLO: You've got the devil in you, sure enough.

GOSLING: The very d-d-devil!

BAZILE: (*Aside.*) So Suzanna and the Count have organised all this without me. See if I care.

FIGARO: As for the rest of you knaves, when you hear me shout, light up the whole area or you'll wish you'd never been born. (*He twists SUNBURN's arm.*)

SUNBURN: (*Running off, screaming.*) That hurts!

BAZILE: Heaven send the bridegroom joy!

(*All exit.*)

FIGARO: Oh women, so feeble! Yet so deceitful! Sooner or later we all show our true self. Yours is to deceive. You refused me so obstinately when I urged you to accept yet the very minute you gave me your word you... And how he smiled when he read the note! What a dupe I've been! Well, my Lord the Count, you shall not have her...no you shan't. Just because you're an aristocrat you think you're a genius! Nobility, a fortune, a position in society, they've all made you so proud. What did you actually do to come by such advantages? Get born! That's all. I'm just one of the crowd. I have had to employ more nous, more ingenuity simply in order to survive than the government would have used to rule Spain for the last hundred years. Yet you want to rival me for her love... Somebody's coming. It's her. No, there's nobody there. (*He sits on a bench.*) The night is as black as the devil and here I sit like a stupid husband when I'm not even half-married. Is there anything stranger than Fate? The son of I don't know whom; stolen by bandits; ran away to become an honest man since when I've been buffeted from pillar to post and repulsed everywhere. I learned chemistry, pharmacology, surgery and the best living the great and the good can afford me is to become a horse doctor. I grew tired of making sick animals sicker so
I tried a completely different career and threw myself headlong into the theatre and nearly broke my neck in the process. I scribbled off a play set in a harem. A Spanish author needn't worry about criticising Mohammed, so I thought, when lo and behold an envoy arrives from God knows where to say that my verses have caused offence in the Ottoman Empire, Persia, parts of the East Indies, the whole of Egypt, the kingdoms of Libya, Tripoli, Tunisia, Algeria and Morocco. My play's consigned to the flames to please a gang of Mullahs not one of whom, I bet, can even read. That didn't quite break my spirit but it laid me very low. I was at death's door. Out of work! Despair might have overtaken me when at last I was put up for a job for which I was qualified. It required

someone with a head for figures. So instead of me they gave it to a dancer. This time I was determined to do away with myself. Providence saved me and returned me to my former position in life. I took up my knapsack, razor and strop leaving the fools to feed off their own dreams and set off to earn a living as a barber, shaving my way from town to town. A great nobleman, Count Almaviva, passing through Seville picks me out. I help him to snatch the young and beautiful Rosina from fat Bartholo and he makes her his Countess. As my reward he tries to bed my fiancée! I am about to fall into an abyss and marry my own mother, when my parents arrive one behind the other just in the nick of time. (*He gets up.*) Arguments rage! It's you, it's him, it's me, it's thee. No it isn't any of us. Well who is it then? (*He sits again.*) How did it all happen to me? Why did destiny single me out for some things and not others? I have to live it out, whether I like it or not. And who is this person I call 'I'? A chance assembly of unknown parts in the pursuit of pleasure and ripe for its enjoyment, doing any kind of job in order to survive: Ambitious from vanity, industrious by necessity, but lazy…with the sheer delight of it all. An orator despite the dangers; a poet for pleasure; a musician when needed; a lover in fits of madness. I've seen it all, done
it all, been it all. My illusions have all been destroyed. Abused and destroyed! Oh Suzie, my Suzie. You're torturing me. Somebody's coming! Now is the moment of decision!

(*He withdraws almost offstage as the COUNTESS, dressed as SUZANNA and SUZANNA, dressed as the COUNTESS enters with MARCELINE.*)

SUZANNA: (*Whispering to the COUNTESS.*) I thought Marceline said that Figaro would be here.

MARCELINE: He is! Keep your voice down.

SUZANNA: One's listening to us and the other's coming to find me. Let's get on with it.

MARCELINE: I don't want to miss a word of this. I'll go and hide in the pavilion. (*She goes into the kiosk where FANCHETTE is hiding.*)

SUZANNA: (*Loud.*) You're shivering my Lady. Are you cold?

COUNTESS: (*Loud.*) It's damp this evening. I think I'll go back to the chateau.

SUZANNA: (*Loud.*) If you don't need me any longer, my Lady, I'd like to stay and take the air for a moment, here under the trees.

COUNTESS: (*Loud.*) Don't catch a chill. There's evening dew.

SUZANNA: (*Loud.*) I'm prepared for it.

FIGARO: (*Aside.*) I bet she is!

(*SUZANNA withdraws to the opposite far side of the stage to FIGARO as CHERUBINO enters singing dressed in his uniform.*)

CHERUBINO: I had a beauteous godmother
One whom I always adored...

COUNTESS: (*Aside.*) The page!

CHERUBINO: (*Stopping.*) There's someone here! I'd better get to my hideaway, Fanchette is waiting... It's a woman!

COUNTESS: Merciful heaven!

CHERUBINO: (*Bending down and looking through the gloom.*) It can't be. From this distance that feathered headress looks awfully like Suzanna's.

COUNTESS: (*Aside.*) Dear God, don't let the Count come now!

(*The COUNT appears upstage.*)

CHERUBINO: (*Approaching and taking the COUNTESS' hand despite her trying to withdraw it.*) It is you Suzie. Your soft hands are trembling. Feel my beating heart.

(*He tries to kiss the back of her hand but she withdraws it.*)

COUNTESS: (*Whispering.*) Go away!

CHERUBINO: Did you come to my hideaway just for me?

COUNTESS: No. Figaro's on his way.

COUNT: (*Aside.*) Is that Suzanna?

CHERUBINO: (*To the COUNTESS.*) He doesn't frighten me. I know you're not waiting for him.

COUNTESS: What do you mean?

COUNT: (*Aside.*) There's somebody with her.

CHERUBINO: I heard it all behind the chair this morning. It's his Lordship you're waiting for.

COUNT: (*Aside.*) It's that damned pageboy!

FIGARO: (*Aside.*) And they say it doesn't pay to eavesdrop.

SUZANNA: (*Aside.*) Little meddler!

COUNTESS: (*To CHERUBINO.*) Please go.

CHERUBINO: Not until I get my reward for being obedient.

COUNTESS: (*Alarmed.*) Reward?

CHERUBINO: Twenty kisses on your own account and a hundred for what I did for your mistress.

COUNTESS: How dare you!

CHERUBINO: Oh I dare! You take her place with the Count. I take his place with you. The only one who loses out is Figaro.

FIGARO: (*Aside.*) Fiend!

SUZANNA: (*Aside.*) The impudence!

(*CHERUBINO tries to kiss the COUNTESS. The COUNT interposes himself and receives the kiss.*)

COUNTESS: Good God!

FIGARO: (*Aside – hearing the kiss.*) What a nice girl I was going to marry!

CHERUBINO: (*Feeling the COUNT's clothes. Aside.*) His Lordship. (*He runs over to the pavilion where FANCHETTE and MARCELINE are hiding and enters.*)

FIGARO: I'd like to…

COUNT: (*Believing he is talking to CHERUBINO.*) Thank you for the kiss! (*He tries to punch him but hits FIGARO instead.*)

FIGARO: Ah!

COUNT: There's one back.

FIGARO: (*Withdrawing upstage and rubbing his cheek.*) Perhaps they were right about eavesdropping!

SUZANNA: (*Laughing.*) Ha, ha, ha!

COUNT: (*To the COUNTESS whom he mistakes for SUZANNA.*) What's the matter with that pageboy? I hit him and he runs off laughing.

FIGARO: (*Aside.*) If it had been him, he'd be in tears.

COUNT: I come across him everywhere I turn! But enough of him. It's spoiling the pleasure of discovering you here.

COUNTESS: (*Imitating SUZANNA.*) Did you think I'd be here?

COUNT: Your message was ingenious and precise. But why are you trembling?

COUNTESS: I was afraid.

COUNT: Let me pass on the pageboy's kiss to you. (*He kisses her on the forehead.*)

COUNTESS: That's naughty.

FIGARO: (*Aside.*) Slut!

SUZANNA: (*Aside.*) She's charming!

COUNT: (*Taking her hand.*) What soft skin you have. I wish the Countess had such fine hands...

COUNTESS: (*Aside.*) Unbelievable!

COUNT: ...or such a firm and rounded arm. Such pretty mischievous fingers...

COUNTESS: This is love talking?

COUNT: Love is a tale told by the heart. Its theme is pleasure and that theme has brought me to my knees.

COUNTESS: Don't you love the Countess any more?

COUNT: Very much, but after three years the marriage has become rather conventional.

COUNTESS: What more do you want from her?

COUNT: The things I find in you, my beauty.

COUNTESS: And what are they?

COUNT: Less conformity. More excitement maybe. Piquant behaviour. Even the occasional no. Our wives think simply loving us is enough. They tell you again and again 'I love you.' Maybe it's true! Maybe. But they're so compliant, so obliging, so willing – always the same adoration until one day one realises that an elegant sufficiency has taken the place of passion and ecstasy.

COUNTESS: (*Aside.*) There's a lesson I shan't forget!

COUNT: Over and over again the thought has struck me that if we look elsewhere for the pleasure that eludes us at home it's because our wives don't understand how to sustain our taste, how to renew our affection, reinvigorate the charm of possessing us by introducing a little variety.

COUNTESS: So it's all down to them is it?

COUNT: You don't expect us to do anything, surely? You can't fight nature. Our job is the hunt, the catch, the win…

COUNTESS: And theirs?

COUNT: Is to keep us hooked. They forget it too easily.

COUNTESS: I shan't.

COUNT: Nor I.

SUZANNA: (*Aside.*) Nor I.

COUNT: (*Taking his wife's hand.*) There's an echo here. Let's keep our voices down. Don't bother your pretty little head about it. You have such loveliness and beauty! A dash of fantasy and you would be the most inspiring of mistresses. (*He kisses her head.*) Suzie, I am a Castillian and my word is my bond. Here is the gold I promised you for the rights that are no longer mine and because the gift you are offering me is priceless, I give you this diamond too. Wear it as a token of your love for me.

COUNTESS: (*Curtseying.*) Suzanna accepts everything.

FIGARO: (*Aside.*) Total depravity.

SUZANNA: (*Aside.*) Keep the gifts coming!

COUNT: (*Aside.*) She's greedy. So much the better.

COUNTESS: I see torches.

COUNT: Just people joining your wedding party. Let's step into this pavilion for a moment and let them pass.

COUNTESS: But it's so dark.

COUNT: (*Gently dragging her.*) We're not going in there to read!

FIGARO: (*Aside.*) She's going in, God damn it! I never thought she'd do that! (*He moves forward.*)

COUNT: (*In a commanding tone.*) Who goes there?

FIGARO: (*Angrily.*) I'm not going anywhere. I'm coming.

COUNT: (*Aside to the COUNTESS.*) It's Figaro! (*He runs off.*)

COUNTESS: I'll follow you later.

(*She goes into the right hand pavilion while the COUNT runs upstage and loses himself in the wood.*)

FIGARO: (*Still believing the COUNTESS is SUZANNA he searches for both of them.*) I can't hear anything now. They've gone in and that's that. (*In an altered tone.*) You husbands who hire private detectives and spend months torturing yourselves with your suspicions, just take my example. Follow your bride around from day one. Keep your ears open and find out everything there is to know about her. I have no suspicions. No doubts. I know exactly where I stand. (*Marching up and down.*) And
I don't mind at all. Her treachery is like water off a duck's back. Anyway, now I've got them. Both of them!

SUZANNA: (*Aside.*) I'll make you pay for your suspicions. (*Imitating the COUNTESS.*) Who's there?

FIGARO: 'Who's there?' Someone who wishes that the plague had finished him at birth.

SUZANNA: Why, it's you Figaro!

FIGARO: My Lady!

SUZANNA: Shhhh! Speak quietly!

FIGARO: Oh my Lady! You've come at the right moment. Do you know where his Excellency is hiding?

SUZANNA: Why should I care?

FIGARO: And do you know where Suzanna is?

SUZANNA: Keep your voice down!

FIGARO: I thought her so virtuous and modest! They're both in there. Shall I call them?

SUZANNA: (*She puts her hand over her mouth and forgets to disguise her voice.*) No, don't!

FIGARO: (*Aside.*) It's Suzie: God damn it!

SUZANNA: (*In the COUNTESS' voice.*) Why are you so upset?

FIGARO: (*Aside.*) She's trying to trick me.

SUZANNA: We must avenge ourselves, Figaro.

FIGARO: Do you really want to?

SUZANNA: I couldn't call myself a woman if I didn't. You men are experts at it.

FIGARO: It's true but even a woman can help. Every little counts.

SUZANNA: (*Aside.*) I'll hit him.

FIGARO: (*Aside.*) That'd be good just before the wedding...

SUZANNA: Vengeance needs a little love to make it spicier.

FIGARO: Sometimes love may not show itself. The servant must know his place.

SUZANNA: It's cruel of you to say so.

FIGARO: (*On his knees with much passion.*) Oh my Lady! How I adore you. Think where we are and at what moment and let your heart forgive my clumsiness.

SUZANNA: (*Aside.*) My hand is itching.

FIGARO: (*Aside.*) My heart is pounding.

SUZANNA: But have you thought this through properly?

FIGARO: Thoroughly.

SUZANNA: Anger and love are both involved…

FIGARO: Then it's time to act. Give me your hand.

SUZANNA: (*In her own voice, slapping him across the face.*) There!

FIGARO: Ouch!

SUZANNA: And the other one.

FIGARO: Owww! My God! You're not beating carpets!

SUZANNA: (*Slapping him with every phrase.*) It's me. Suzanna, you fool! There's one for your suspicion. One for your revenge. One for your treachery, your scheming, your impudence and your plots. Is this your love? Is this what you meant this morning?

FIGARO: (*Laughing.*) This is love! It's joy! Pure joy and delight! Figaro's over the moon! Slap away, my darling, slap away and when I'm black and blue all over you'll be looking at the luckiest man ever to have been beaten by a woman.

SUZANNA: The luckiest? You lying toad! You seduced the Countess so expertly that I forgot who I was for a moment and fell for you.

FIGARO: Oh I knew who you really were. I couldn't mistake that voice.

SUZANNA: (*Laughing.*) You knew all the time! I shall have to get my own back!

FIGARO: Women! Beat a fellow half to death and still bear a grudge! But you've got some explaining to do! How come you are here when I thought you were with him? And why are you dressed like that? It proves you're innocent but…

SUZANNA: You're the innocent! You walked straight into the trap we'd laid for someone else. It's not our fault that we got two birds with one stone.

FIGARO: We? Who's the other?

SUZANNA: His wife.

FIGARO: His wife?

SUZANNA: That's what I said.

FIGARO: How didn't I guess that. His own wife! Women are infinitely subtle. So the kisses I heard coming from here?

SUZANNA: …landed on her Ladyship.

FIGARO: And the pageboys' kisses?

SUZANNA: (*Laughing.*) On his Excellency!

FIGARO: And this morning from behind the armchair?

SUZANNA: Nobody got those.

FIGARO: Are you sure?

SUZANNA: Do you want another slap?

FIGARO: They're like jewels! I treasure them. But surely the Count's kiss was in earnest.

SUZANNA: Right. On your knees!

FIGARO: I deserve it! I prostrate myself. Belly on the ground.

SUZANNA: The poor Count! He's gone to so much trouble…

FIGARO: (*Getting up.*) …to win his own wife.

(*The COUNT appears upstage and goes straight to the right hand pavilion.*)

COUNT: (*To himself.*) I can't find her anywhere. Perhaps she went in here.

SUZANNA: (*To FIGARO in a whisper.*) It's him!

COUNT: Suzie, are you there?

FIGARO: He's looking for you, so…?

SUZANNA: He hasn't recognised her.

FIGARO: Shall we play? (*He kisses her hand.*)

COUNT: A man on his knees to the Countess; I'm unarmed. Damn!

FIGARO: (*Disguising his voice.*) Forgive me my Lady, I didn't realise that our next tryst would take place on the wedding night.

COUNT: (*Aside.*) The man in the dressing room this morning.

FIGARO: But let it not be an obstacle between us and our pleasure.

COUNT: (*Aside.*) Death, destruction and damnation!

FIGARO: (*Leading her towards the pavilion, to SUZANNA.*) He's getting angry. (*Loud.*) Come, my Lady, and make up for what we missed when I had to leap from the window.

COUNT: (*Aside.*) So!

SUZANNA: (*Near to the left-hand pavilion.*) Before we go in, let's just make sure we haven't been followed. (*FIGARO kisses her forehead.*)

COUNT: Vengeance!

(*SUZANNA runs into the pavilion. The COUNT seizes FIGARO by the arm.*)

FIGARO: Master!

COUNT: You, you villain! Help! Help somebody!

PEDRILLO: (*Entering in his riding boots.*) Ah my Lord. At last.

COUNT: Pedrillo. Thank God. Only you?!

PEDRILLO: Just got back from Seville, sir. Disembowelled the horse.

COUNT: Come over here and make as much noise as you can.

PEDRILLO: (*Shouting.*) I couldn't find the page boy. Here's your package back.

COUNT: (*Pushing him away.*) Stop shouting you imbecile.

PEDRILLO: You told me to make a lot of noise.

COUNT: To attract attention you fool. Hello. Can't anyone hear me? I'm over here!

PEDRILLO: You've already got Figaro and me. How many do you want?

(*GOSLING, BAZILE, BARTHOLO, ANTONIO and SUNBURN enter.*)

BARTHOLO: (*To FIGARO.*) You called. We came running.

COUNT: (*Indicating the left-hand pavilion.*) Guard that door.

BAZILE: (*Aside to FIGARO.*) Did you catch him with Suzanna?

COUNT: (*Pointing to FIGARO.*) All of you surround this man and guard him with your lives.

BAZILE: Ha! Ha!

COUNT: (*Furious.*) Shut up! (*To FIGARO.*) Now, you wretch, will you answer my questions?

FIGARO: How could I refuse, my Lord. You're in control of everything here, except yourself.

COUNT: Except myself?

ANTONIO: Clearly!

COUNT: (*Controlling himself.*) I can't stand his calm tone.

FIGARO: I'm not a soldier. I'm not paid to be killed for reasons I don't know. I want to know my offence.

COUNT: (*Beside himself with rage.*) Monstrous! How can you pretend you don't know! Perhaps you'd do me the kindness to tell me the name of the Lady you brought to this pavilion?

FIGARO: (*Pointing to the right hand one.*) Do you mean that one?

COUNT: No. This one.

FIGARO: Oh this one! I see. Just a young lady who has done me the honour to show me her affection.

BAZILE: (*Astounded.*) Ah ha!

COUNT: Did you hear that gentlemen?

BARTHOLO: (*Astounded.*) We did!

COUNT: And are this Lady's affections committed elsewhere that you know of?

FIGARO: There's a certain nobleman who has been after her for some time but either because he's neglected her too often or because she's fonder of me than this great man, today she honoured me with her company.

COUNT: When a man's dishonour is flaunted in front of the world he has a right to public vengeance. (*He goes into the pavilion.*)

ANTONIO: He's right!

GOSLING: Who's pinched whose wife?

FIGARO: (*Laughing.*) Nobody yet!

(*The COUNT enters from the pavilion dragging someone behind him that we can't see.*)

COUNT: Don't even try to protest your innocence. It's all over. Your time's up! It's as well we have no children…

FIGARO: Cherubino!

COUNT: The page!

BAZILE: Ha! Ha!

COUNT: (*Aside.*) That devil pageboy again! (*To CHERUBINO.*) What were you doing in there?

CHERUBINO: You told me to stay out of sight.

PEDRILLO: For this I nearly killed my horse.

COUNT: Antonio, go in and drag out that strumpet! Let the wicked creature stand before her judge.

GOSLING: Does he think her Ladyship's in there?

ANTONIO: It would serve him right if she were! Sauce for the goose!

COUNT: (*Furious.*) At once!

(*ANTONIO goes into the pavilion.*)

Gentlemen, you will now see that the pageboy was not alone.

CHERUBINO: My tension was unbearable. She was only trying to relieve it.

ANTONIO: (*Dragging someone behind him by the arm.*) Come on out! We all know why you went in there.

FIGARO: .My little cousin!

BAZILE: Ha ha!

COUNT: Fanchette!

ANTONIO: I don't believe it! Very clever of your Lordship to let me show the whole village that it was my daughter who's been causing all this trouble.

COUNT: How was I to know she was in there! I… (*He makes to go in himself.*)

BARTHOLO: Allow me Count. I am totally calm. (*He goes in.*)

GOSLING: This is complicated.

BARTHOLO: Don't be afraid. Nobody's going to hurt you, I promise. (*He sees her.*) Marceline!

BAZILE: Ha ha!

FIGARO: (*Laughing.*) This is better than I thought. My mother's in there too!

ANTONIO: Oh no, please!

COUNT: (*Outraged.*) I'm not interested in her. Where's the Countess?

(*SUZANNA enters with her fan covering her face.*)

COUNT: At last! (*He seizes her violently by the arm.*) Gentlemen, what punishment do you think this odious creature deserves?

(*SUZANNA falls on her knees at his feet.*)

Oh don't try that one!

(*FIGARO falls to his knees on the other side of the COUNT.*)

You're wasting your time.

(*MARCELINE falls to her knees.*)

The answer's no.

(*They all fall to their knees except GOSLING.*)

And it would be if there were a hundred of you! No! No! No!

COUNTESS: (*Entering from the other pavilion and throwing herself on her knees.*) Would my plea make a difference?

COUNT: (*Looking from SUZANNA to the COUNTESS.*) What? What are you…?

GOSLING: It's her Ladyship!

COUNT: (*Trying to raise her.*) Where…who…oh! (*In a tone of supplication.*) Only the most generous act of forgiveness on your part could…

COUNTESS: If it were you, you'd say, 'No, definitely not.' But for the third time today I forgive you unconditionally.

SUZANNA: And so do I.

MARCELINE: So do I.

FIGARO: So do I. There is an echo here!

COUNT: An echo! I tried to be clever and they've treated me like a child.

COUNTESS: Don't be too upset, my Lord.

FIGARO: It's all good training for a future ambassador.

COUNT: (*To SUZANNA.*) That note with the pin?

SUZANNA: Her Ladyship dictated it.

COUNT: Then I shall reply to her. (*He kisses her hand.*)

COUNTESS: Everyone shall have his own. (*She gives a purse to FIGARO and a diamond to SUZANNA.*)

SUZANNA: Another dowry.

FIGARO: That makes three. This one took some getting.

SUZANNA: Like our marriage?

SUNBURN: Can I have the bride's lucky garter?

COUNTESS: (*Takes the ribbon from her bodice and throws it to the ground.*) There it is. It was with her clothes.

(*The village boys scramble to pick it up. CHERUBINO gets it first.*)

CHERUBINO: Anyone who wants it will have to fight me for it.

COUNT: (*Laughing.*) Would you like another smack like the one I gave you earlier?

CHERUBINO: You smacked me?!

FIGARO: In my face! Thus the mighty dispense justice.

COUNT: Your face? What do you think of that Countess?

COUNTESS: (*Dreaming.*) Yes, my dear Count, for ever and ever. I swear.

COUNT: And you Justice Gosling. What do you think?

GOSLING: Considering all the evidence, my Lord… I… I… don't quite understand!

ALL: A good verdict.

FIGARO: When I was poor, people despised me. When I prospered, they hated me. Now with a pretty wife and a fortune…

BARTHOLO: People will come flocking to be your friend.

FIGARO: Do you really think so?

BARTHOLO: I know they will.

FIGARO: (*To the audience.*) Leave my wife and fortune alone, but come and celebrate *at last* the marriage of Figaro.

(*All join in singing and dancing.*)

MARCELINE: Married men think vows a joke.
Why should they obey the yoke?
But if their wives a fancy take
To hop the bed and merry-make
Descends the strong arm of man's law
The will of men it serves for sure
It's been the same for ever more.
It's been the same for ever more.

BAZILE: Birth's accident doth separate
Prince from pauper, such is fate.
Life's enterprise pulls each apart
For some the palace, some the hearth.
Some praise the king for his allure,
But monarchies will die for sure
Free spirit's all that can endure.
Free spirit's all that can endure.

FIGARO: The author's words, precisely given,
    To learn exactly we have striven
    To show life from his point of view
    For what he says is all too true
    The rich still reign, their hold is strong
    It's then and now the same old song
    It's then and now the same old song.

The End.

Printed in the USA
CPSIA information can be obtained
at www.ICGtesting.com
LVHW020956171024
794056LV00004B/1166

9 781840 023770